To Jonathan —

Inspire
Creative
Success!

creative

SUCCESS
NOW

Fondly, Astrid

How Creatives Can Thrive
in the 21st Century

ASTRID BAUMGARDNER, JD

INDIE BOOKS
INTERNATIONAL

No part of this publication may be reproduced or distributed in any form or by any means without the prior permission of the publisher. Requests for permission should be directed to permissions@indiebooksintl.com, or mailed to Permissions, Indie Books International, 2424 Vista Way, Suite 316, Oceanside, CA 92054.

The views and opinions in this book are those of the author at the time of writing this book, and do not reflect the opinions of Indie Books International or its editors.

Neither the publisher nor the author is engaged in rendering legal, tax or other professional services through this book. The information is for business education purposes only. If expert assistance is required, the services of appropriate professionals should be sought. The publisher and the author shall have neither liability nor responsibility to any person or entity with respect to any loss or damage caused directly or indirectly by the information in this publication.

ISBN-10: 1-947480-74-X
ISBN-13: 978-1-947480-74-2
Library of Congress Control Number: 2019913121

The Creative Success Now Methodology™ is a pending trademark of Astrid Baumgardner.
Nanopuncture™ is a pending trademark of Dr. Clayton Shiu.
Grammy® is a registered trademark of the National Academy of Recording Arts & Sciences, Inc.
CrossFit® is a registered trademark of CrossFit, Inc.

Thank you to Franklin Covey Co. for permission to use the Covey Matrix© Stephen R. Covey, *The 7 Habits of Highly Effective People: Powerful Lessons in Personal Change* (New York: Free Press, 2004).

The Creative Career Options Circle and the Creative Life Balance Circle were inspired by my coach training program, iPEC, the Institute for Professional Excellence in Coaching and contain my interpretation of the copyrighted work of Bruce D. Schneider and iPEC.

Disclaimer about coaching: The principles in this book are based on my experience as a trained, certified professional coach. Coaching is a modality that helps bring out your inner wisdom so that you can create and live the life of your dreams. Coaching is not therapy and is not designed to cure physical or mental disabilities or illnesses. Coaching may complement therapy but is not a substitute for professional mental health care or medical care.

Designed by Joni McPherson, mcphersongraphics.com

INDIE BOOKS INTERNATIONAL, LLC
2424 VISTA WAY, SUITE 316
OCEANSIDE, CA 92054
www.indiebooksintl.com

TABLE OF CONTENTS

PROLOGUE

There is a lot of confusion surrounding creativity and creatives, the people who make it happen. So, let's begin by getting clear on the meaning of these terms.

Creativity is the process of generating and actualizing ideas that are new to you and solving problems in a new way.

The MacArthur Foundation, which each year awards its *genius grants*, broadly defines creativity as follows:

> *Creativity comprises the drive and ability to make something new or to connect the seemingly unconnected in significant ways so as to enrich our understanding of ourselves, our communities, the world, and the universe that we inhabit. Creativity can take many forms: asking questions that open onto fields of inquiry as yet unexplored; developing innovative solutions to perplexing problems; inventing novel methods, tools, or art forms; fusing ideas from different disciplines into wholly new constructions; producing works that broaden the horizons of the imagination.[1]*

Who Are The Creatives?

Creatives are problem solvers, whether it is a problem of how to fill the empty canvas, the empty page, or the empty stage. Creatives thrive on new ideas and, according to the MacArthur Foundation, possess the "ability to transcend traditional boundaries, willingness to take risks, persistence in the face of personal and conceptual obstacles, capacity to synthesize disparate ideas and approaches."[2]

Positive psychologist Mihalyi Csikszentmihalyi, who has studied creativity, explains that creatives possess seemingly contradictory characteristics that can be summarized as follows:

> *Energetic, yet often quiet and at rest*
> *Smart, yet naïve*
> *Playful yet disciplined and persevering*
> *Imaginative yet realistic*
> *Extroverted and introverted*
> *Humble, yet proud*
> *Flexible in gender roles*
> *Rebellious yet conservative*
> *Passionate, yet objective about their work*
> *Open and sensitive, experiencing suffering yet also a great deal of enjoyment.*[3]

These inherent contradictions suggest why creatives have the capacity to see things in a different way and come up with new solutions.

If this sounds like you, keep reading.

CHAPTER ONE

Debunking The Creative Myths

Creativity matters to our world. Once thought of as a nice (but not necessary) characteristic limited to the realm of artists, creativity is now recognized as an essential twenty-first-century skill set. Creativity involves complex thinking to generate novel solutions that make our world a better place. Creatives work hard because what they do really matters to them and they love what they do. And many opportunities exist in today's world to make a living and thrive in the twenty-first century.

This book lays out a three-part *Creative Success Now* Methodology consisting of the mindset, authenticity set, and skill sets that can empower you to pursue the creative life—both for your personal journey toward success *and* because the world needs your ideas. Ultimately, this book will help you to solve the many problems you encounter as a creative person so that you can live as a successful creative in the twenty-first century.

Let's start off by debunking four of the top myths about creativity and creative people.

MYTH NUMBER ONE:
Creativity Is Only For Artists

For many people, creativity is siphoned off to the arts. It's easy to see why: A great painting, an inspirational piece of music, an exquisite ballet: these are clear manifestations of new ideas. But creativity is a lot more than inspiration for the arts.

Reality: Creativity is an essential, wide-ranging, twenty-first-century skill.

Welcome to the twenty-first century. We live in a time of change, uncertainty, and enormous opportunity.

We have evolved from the agrarian age to the industrial age and now to the information age, in which digital and communications technologies have made it possible to access enormous stores of information and communicate rapidly, without boundaries. And these technologies are upending many traditional institutions while giving rise to a whole new economy.

This is where creativity comes in, because creativity—the problem-solving process of generating and actualizing new ideas—is a highly-valued skill in today's world and creatives can be found in many different parts of our culture.

THE CREATIVITY SKILL

For starters, creativity is now recognized as a critical skill for the twenty-first-century workforce.

A 2010 IBM survey of 1,500 global CEOs revealed that creativity was the number one skill required to navigate the uncertainties of the global economy.[1]

The World Economic Forum now cites creativity as the third most important skill that companies want for their employees and recruits in the next five years.[2]

THE CREATIVE CLASS

And while creativity resides in our artists, musicians, designers, and writers, it extends well beyond the arts to many sectors where actualizing new ideas is critical to success.

Richard Florida has coined the term *The Creative Class* to describe the people who create "new ideas, new technologies or creative content." The creative class spans design, education, arts, music, and entertainment, but also extends to scientists and engineers, university professors, poets, and architects. The creative class in the United States is estimated to comprise one-third of the workforce, numbered at forty million people and growing.[3]

Indeed, the MacArthur genius grants have been awarded to writers, scientists, artists, lawyers, social scientists, humanists, teachers, and entrepreneurs.

CREATIVES ARE EVERYWHERE

What does this mean to you as a creative?

Just about anyone can be a creative. In my work, I have helped not only musicians and composers but also arts leaders, lawyers, designers, entrepreneurs, journalists, and business, marketing, and advertising executives. Indeed, throughout this book, you will hear stories of success from the realm of the arts and beyond.

Bottom line: While creativity may have once be seen as a "nice but not necessary" quality found only in artists, it is a vital part of today's world.

MYTH NUMBER TWO:
The *Eureka!* Moment

Another pervasive myth around creativity is the *Eureka!* or *Aha!* Moment: that creativity is a burst-of-genius idea.

Icons of the *Eureka!* Moment abound:

- **Isaac Newton** developing the theory of gravity while sitting under a tree and getting hit on the head with an apple (Reality: The discovery took years, and evidence of the apple is sketchy).[4]

- **Wolfgang Amadeus Mozart** producing his symphonies in one brilliant sweep of genius (Reality: Mozart's creative process was nuanced and labored).[5]

- **Thomas Edison's** invention of the light bulb (Reality: Edison built upon the work of many predecessors).[6]

Indeed, we tend to romanticize creative genius. That is understandable, because the public only sees the end product of creativity, not the process.

Reality: Creativity involves hard work and multiple cognitive processes.

In fact, creativity is not just a burst of brilliant ideas arising out of nowhere. Research on, and the practice of, creativity tell another story; one of complexity, nonlinear messiness, in order to liberate the imagination and come up with new solutions.

Having a great idea is just the start of a creative process. Creativity involves defining the right problem to solve, experimenting, risk-taking, reframing, developing ideas, putting ideas together in new ways, incubating to leave time for ideas to evolve and mature, and refining the product until it is just right.

What about the right-brain versus left-brain distinction? Not so fast.

Research from neuroscience confirms that creativity involves both sides of the brain, with a complex chain of connections. As explained in *Scientific American*, the creative process involves many different brain regions that interact both consciously and unconsciously, along with different emotions.[7]

Creativity is "messy," according to researcher Scott Barry Kaufman, scientific director of The Imagination Institute in the Positive Psychol-

 Another pervasive myth around creativity is the *Eureka!* or *Aha!* Moment: that creativity is a burst-of-genius idea.

ogy Center at the University of Pennsylvania.[8] Dr. Kaufman goes on to explain that creative people exhibit tremendous cognitive flexibility and can "juggle seemingly contradictory modes of thought—cognitive and emotional, deliberate and spontaneous."[9]

When you talk to creative people, you hear a mix of intuition, idea-generating, hard-core problem-solving, and risk. Pulitzer-prize winning composer David Lang views creativity as "solving problems" to create something that has never existed before. Lang observes that creatives can never become complacent and must put out their ideas with as much commitment and strength as possible. "I like the risk, knowing that [in order to create], I have to use my wits."[10]

For award-winning composer Reena Esmail, a composer's job is not to find answers, but to find the next questions. This involves deeply intentional, consistent creative engagement. Esmail writes every single day because she knows she has "very little control over what comes into my mind, or over the result of my work. I only have control over how much time I spend creating."[11]

In an attempt to harness the messiness of creativity, multiple processes exist to encourage the fruition of new ideas. These include design thinking, now taught at Stanford's famous d. school and creativity problem-solving, the subject of a master of science in creative studies at the SUNY Buffalo[12, 13,]. My class at Yale University's School of Music blends these processes to help my students generate innovative solutions to the big problems facing classical music today.[14]

And even with these processes, creativity is still the result of cognitive and emotional messiness and complexity.

Bottom Line: In short, creatives work hard to get it right.

MYTH NUMBER THREE:
The Mad, Miserable Artist

A corollary to the myth of the genius creative is the myth of the mad, miserable genius: that creative genius goes hand-in-hand with mental illness.

Think Vincent Van Gogh, cutting off his ear and languishing in an insane asylum in the South of France.

Or Michael Jackson, with his many eccentricities.

Or tortured souls, like Sylvia Plath and Virginia Woolf, who ultimately committed suicide.

But is this so? Are creative people mad and miserable?

Reality: Creativity can promote happiness and well-being.

While there is some association between mental illness and the creation of art, research from positive psychology indicates that creativity contributes to a sense of well-being and happiness.[15] Positive psychology is the study of human flourishing and what makes us happy, with happiness defined by positive psychology researcher Sonja Lyubomirsky as "the experience of joy, contentment, or positive well-being, combined with a sense that one's life is good, meaningful, and worthwhile."[16] As we will see, creativity promotes positive emotions and correlates with several other measures of happiness.

CREATIVITY AND POSITIVE EMOTIONS

Creativity feels good. In fact, the research shows that people who engage in creative activities experience positive emotions. In one study, people who participated in everyday creativity like cooking and writing reported that they were happy and energized when engaging in these activities.[17]

Another study shows that being in a positive mood helps you to be more creative in your thinking.[18]

CREATIVITY AND FLOW

Another link between creativity and happiness is flow.

Flow is the state of optimal experience described by psychologist Mihalyi Csikszentmihalyi as the total immersion in a complex activity of creation that you are intrinsically motivated to pursue where your skill level meets the challenge at hand and time goes by to the point that you do not even notice.[19]

And when you experience that zone, flow gives rise to happiness.[20]

CREATIVITY AND RESILIENCE

Did you know that the chances of winning a job with a major orchestra—a grueling process in which hundreds of musicians audition before a panel of judges behind a blind screen to perfectly execute lots of short musical excerpts with the hope of winning one coveted seat in that orchestra—have been described as lower than the chances of entering the NBA?[21]

So, why do so many musicians continue to audition for orchestra jobs, despite the slim odds of making it, and the many rounds of rejection they face?

Because of their calling and their capacity for resilience—another aspect of happiness.

In a longitudinal study of musicians, psychologist Sasha Dubrow found that musicians were incredibly resilient in the face of the challenges they face in their careers because they experienced their careers as a "calling," or the pursuit of one's passion.[22]

CREATIVITY AND SENSE OF PURPOSE

What do musicians at Yale, arts leaders in the opera world and creative business executives looking to transition to work in the *do-gooder space*—three groups with whom I have worked— have in common?

As creatives, they are fueled by a sense of purpose.

Creativity is "full-blast living," in the words of Mihalyi Csikszent-mihalyi, who goes on to say that:

"Of all human activities, *creativity* comes closest to providing the fulfillment we all hope to get in our lives....Creativity is a central source of meaning in our lives. Most of the things that are interesting, important, and human are the result of creativity."[23]

This is another attribute of well-being in life that creative people possess: working toward meaningful goals that they are intrinsically motivated to achieve.[24] That's why arts graduates report deep satisfaction from their creative education and pursuit of professional work.[25]

Bottom Line: No wonder creatives work so hard. What they do really matters to them, and they love what they do.

MYTH NUMBER FOUR:
The Starving Artist

Many people still think of the starving artists in *La Bohème* and *Rent* as the model for making one's living as a creative artist. As in, you can't.

Why are so many parents loathe to let their children major in the arts?

Why the emphasis in higher education on STEM disciplines (science, technology, engineering, and mathematics) to the detriment of the humanities?

My answer: The fear that one cannot make a sustainable living in the arts.

To add to this fear, crafting a career in the creative sector often does not follow a linear path to success. Yet today, it is not just creative careers that do not afford readily accessible career paths. Many professions are suffering from an oversupply of qualified candidates and a diminishing demand, whether it's tenure-track university teaching, classical music, or even my former profession, the law.[26]

And in today's complicated, wired, fast-moving world, many traditional career paths—from the recording industry to traditional publishing to media—are in decline due to the myriad changes ushered in by the digital revolution and free access to information through the internet.[27]

Reality: A closer look at our economy reveals another story. In fact, creatives are able to make a living in today's economy.

THE CREATIVE ECONOMY

Not surprisingly, with creativity as an essential twenty-first-century skill, we now speak of the creative economy. Recognized as a significant force in the world economy, the creative economy encompasses advertising, architecture, arts and crafts, design, fashion, film, video, photography, music, performing arts, publishing, research and development, software, computer games, electronic publishing, and TV/radio.[28]

Another study shows that globally, eleven creative industry sectors have generated $2,250 billion in revenues (3 percent of world GDP) and accounted for 29.5 million jobs, or 1 percent of the world's active population.[29]

On a practical level, there are many good jobs for creative thinkers, ranging from the arts to the sciences and the tech world, with 46 percent of arts graduates earning over $50,000/year. [30, 31]

OPPORTUNITIES FROM THE DIGITAL REVOLUTION

While the digital revolution has eliminated jobs, it has created other opportunities for creative people.[32] It's time to get rid of the "false binary between pro-technology optimistic futurism and anti-technology digital pessimism."[33]

The digital revolution means that there are more options out there for creative people.[34] In the music business, you can still have a label release your recording, but digital technologies make it possible to write, distribute, market, promote, and access music without the need for intermediaries. The result has been new ways to generate revenue as a musician.[35] Filmmakers can reach their audiences through YouTube and Vimeo in addition to working with studios, and authors can choose to publish their books with both traditional and independent publishers, along with Amazon and e-books. Creatives freelance and have portfolio careers, assembling work from teaching, performing, writing, and selling their creative content through expert services, products, and merchandise. And thanks to their flexible ways of thinking and solving problems, creatives have a leg up in spotting opportunities and creating their own career paths.

The caveat here is that many of these digital opportunities are not especially lucrative, which means that creatives need to juggle many different professional opportunities and revenue streams. Yet those who are committed to using their creativity are finding ways to make it work.

Throughout this book, you will find many examples of creatives who are living a wonderful life from their creativity.

Bottom Line: The digital revolution has fundamentally changed the twenty-first-century workplace, and creatives can take advantage of many opportunities for making a living and contributing to the global creative economy.

GOOD NEWS FOR CREATIVES

Creativity is a highly valued skill set that drives a significant portion of the global economy. It does not depend on a random stroke of genius, but instead on inspired hard work that creatives dive into, fueled by a sense of purpose and meaning with the potential for well-being and happiness—and a job that pays.

So, for all of you out there who thrive on your ideas, work hard to get your ideas out into the world, are driven by a sense of purpose to create meaning from your creative work and want to thrive in the twenty-first century: This book is for you.

CHAPTER TWO

Your Creative Success Road Map

This book is here to guide you to creative success with a methodology that is grounded in the principles of positive psychology. To give you a sense of how positive psychology relates to your creative success, here's one tantalizing truth revealed by research:

Happiness breeds success.

That's right.

Perhaps you believe that you will only be happy when you achieve your milestone goal of getting tenure at a prestigious university, publishing a bestseller, or making a million dollars. The research shows otherwise. When you are happy and optimistic and experience positive emotions, you are able to cultivate the kind of mindset and engage in behaviors that give rise to greater success and fulfillment. In other words, success flows from happiness.[1]

The Advantages Of Being Happy

There are well-documented advantages to being happy and experiencing positive emotions.

Positive emotions make it possible to be more creative, thoughtful, and open to new ideas. When we feel positive, our brains are flooded with feel-good chemicals like dopamine and serotonin, which in turn help us to work more effectively, organize and retrieve information more quickly, and become more skilled at complex analysis and problem-solving.

People who experience positive emotions are less stressed and physically healthier. In the workplace, people who experience positive emotions are more productive, make more effective leaders, and enjoy higher performance ratings, higher salaries, and greater job security.

Moreover, 40 percent of your capacity to be happy is within your control and depends on your own behavior.[2] The *Creative Success Now* Methodology provides you with many tools and strategies that help to change your mindset and behavior and lead you to experience greater happiness—and success.

The *Creative Success Now* Methodology

With these principles in mind, here is the *Creative Success Now* methodology in a nutshell.

Part I
The *Creative Success Now* Mindset

- **Persevere with the Growth Mindset.** The journey to success starts by adopting the *Creative Success Now* mindset. The first aspect of this mindset is perseverance: the drive to build on your talent and intelligence by taking risks, persisting, and bouncing back in the face of challenge and setbacks and learning from your mistakes.

- **Get in the Flow with Positivity and Proactivity.** You will continue to build the *Creative Success Now* mindset by embracing positivity to find your flow and proactivity by taking the initiative and creating your own opportunities.

PART II
The *Creative Success Now* Authenticity Set

- **Play to Your Passions and Strengths.** Next, you will delve into defining your authentic self, starting with passion and strengths. You will learn how to tap into the power of your passions—the energy that inspires creativity—and to play to your strengths—the natural gifts that you proactively apply to maximize your talents.

- **Align with Your Values and Your Purpose.** You will continue to define your authentic self by finding and aligning with your values—the principles that run your life—and your life purpose—how you create meaning and put your talents and passions to work to make the world a better place.

PART III
The *Creative Success Now* Skill Sets

- **Commit to Creative Goal Achievement.** The next step is to build key skill sets for achieving creative success. First, you will learn how to make your dreams come to pass by creating inspiring goals, breaking down your goals into manageable steps, and making a realistic action plan.

- **Overcome the Creativity Killers.** To help you when you hit a wall and feel that working toward that big dream seems impossible, you will learn how to overcome the three top obstacles to creative success: perfectionism, fear, and compare-and-despair.

- **Master the Principles of Creative Time Management.** To help you manage the many different balls that you juggle as a creative, you will discover a system for focusing on your important work and setting your priorities according-ly, along with a host of tools for managing your time and your energy.

- **Create Your Personal Brand.** Now it's time to connect with the greater world. You will learn how to stand out from the crowd and connect with the people you are meant to help by creating your personal brand.

- **Engage in Effective and Effortless Networking.** You will learn the secrets of effective and effortless networking to build your mutually supportive circle of professional friends.

- **Sustain Your Creative Success.** To sustain your creative success, learn the three principles of financial management and create your support team.

> BONUS: To continue on your creative success journey, Appendices D and E lay out an ongoing system to help you keep track of your progress and recharge your creative life with strategies of innovation.

To assess where you currently are in your creative journey, download the Creative Success Roadmap from my website at creativesuccessnow.com/CreativeSuccessRoadmap.

My Creative Journey

My journey started twelve years ago when I almost died. I would never have predicted the outcome.

On March 5, 2007, I had a small outpatient procedure. Just thirty-six hours later, I was lying on the floor of the emergency room at New York-Presbyterian/Weill Cornell Hospital with sepsis—a rampant infection with an over 50 percent mortality rate.

For five days, my life hung in the balance. I had four major surgeries and was in a coma for ten days. Then, on my birthday, March 16, I woke up from the coma. I was a true mess: I couldn't walk, talk, eat, or use my hands—but I knew that I had come back for a reason.

Before that, I felt I was cruising along. I had been a successful partner in two law firms, the former deputy executive director of the French Institute Alliance Française of New York City, and a partner in a start-up. I was consulting to nonprofit arts boards and studying at Juilliard, not to mention embracing being the mother of two great kids with a wonderful husband and friends, a daily exercise routine, and an active cultural life.

After I recovered from sepsis and was discharged from my month-long hospital stay, my productive life was transformed into one of rehab, physical therapy, and another major surgery.

In October 2007, as I was lying on my couch recovering from surgery number five, I heard a voice that said, "Astrid, you need to get up from that couch and help people with their difficult life transitions."

That's how I discovered life coaching: a way to share positivity and courage and help people transition to a better life. I decided to dedicate

Just thirty-six hours after a small outpatient procedure, I was lying on the floor of the emergency room at New York-Presbyterian/Weill Cornell Hospital with sepsis—a rampant infection with an over 50 percent mortality rate.

my life to coaching creatives because what they do matters to making our world a better place.

Within a month of discovering life coaching, I signed up for coaching school, and six months later, started my coaching business, working with creative lawyers and early-stage professional musicians. I also discovered my passion for teaching. Soon, I was doing career workshops at Juilliard. Whatever I didn't know, I researched and studied. I solicited feedback, information, and guidance from friends and colleagues. I experimented with different teaching techniques and workshop ideas, and I practiced coaching and teaching on pretty much anyone who would listen. Along the way, not only did I develop a great business, but I also discovered that I, too, was a creative.

In 2010, I was invited to guest lecture at the Yale School of Music, a graduate school within Yale University, and a year later, I joined the faculty and administrative staff to create our school's Office of Career Strategies. I've been there ever since, teaching and coaching the next generation of brilliant musicians and passionate cultural leaders. My business has extended to guest lecturing at leading music conservatories and arts leadership training programs, as well as to career transition programs. And I continue to work with individual musicians, arts leaders, and creative professionals to help them achieve their visions of success.

Creating your success builds on what you as a creative already know how to do: work hard to solve a problem in a new way. You have the inner gifts to ride the wave of transition and confusion that characterize our world. This book will show you that you can succeed in the twenty-first century as a creative by tapping into your inner gifts and following this book's methodology to empower yourself to success.

I am privileged to teach and coach world-class professional and pre-professional musicians, brilliant arts leaders, entrepreneurs, and creative business professionals. When my students and clients incorporate the principles that I lay out in this book, I have seen a shift in their energy that inspires and empowers them to get their creative work out in the world so that the world can benefit from their vision.

That's the process. So, let's get started.

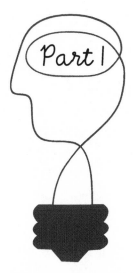

The *Creative Success Now* Mindset

Mindset is the starting point for a successful creative career in today's world.

My friend Adam Sliwinski, a member of the successful percussion quartet Sō Percussion, tells his wife every morning when he wakes up, "Someone has to get up every day and make new music!"[1]

Adam is fueled by passion and positivity. He and his three ensemble members worked tirelessly to create the success of Sō Percussion. And they proactively created their opportunities, going from young, hungry graduate students to the ensemble in residence at Princeton University, heading up their own summer percussion school, and performing around the world in prestigious venues like New York's Carnegie Hall and London's Barbican Centre. In short, they—along with many other creatives whom you will meet in this book—exemplify the kind of mindset that can lead to creative success.

Mindset is your attitude and how you perceive the world based on your experiences. Your mindset is how you feel about your ability to translate your creative talent into a successful career. Your mindset develops based on your experience. The more success you encounter, the more you perceive the world as a place that welcomes success, and the more likely you are to believe in your ability to create success. Conversely, if you have experienced multiple setbacks and have had trouble pushing through your challenges, your perception of the world is likely to be less positive.

For creatives, having the right mindset is essential to success. That mindset is shaped by three elements:

- Persevering through setbacks and learning from your challenges

- Tapping into your best self and finding your flow

- Proactively taking actions and creating opportunities to build toward your success

The good news is that you can develop the *Creative Success Now* mindset. In the next two chapters, you will meet successful creatives who learned how to persevere, find flow, and be proactive in the face of their obstacles to creative success.

CHAPTER THREE

Persevere With The Growth Mindset

I wish you could have been there the day I met Igor Lichtmann. It was September 2016 in my office at the Yale School of Music, a week before classes started. Igor was an ambitious guitar player from Germany who was about to start his second master's program at Yale. He was taking my class and wanted to meet with me to talk about his career options.

Igor was really talented. He began his musical career by forming his own metal band that toured around Europe. In his early twenties, he switched to classical guitar, and he already had a master's degree from a prestigious school in Salzburg, Austria.

But Igor was at a crossroads. He was terrified of failing as a classical musician. Because of his late start in the classical world, he felt he was already behind his peers, and he was afraid to accept certain concert engagements or enter many competitions because he never felt good enough. To make matters worse, he worried that he would never find his place in the classical music world and that he would get stuck in a rut.

"I'm only at Yale for two years, and I don't want to waste any time," he told me. "If I graduate from Yale and the only thing I can do is return to Europe and teach guitar to high school kids, I will feel like my life is a failure. What's out there for musicians besides teaching or doing competitions if I want a good lifestyle?"

"That depends on you. What do you wish you could be doing?" I asked Igor.

He told me that he wanted to live well, doing something in the music world. Then his eyes lit up as he said, "Maybe I could even create my own music company someday. But I don't know much about business, and I have no idea how to create a company."

So, I laid it out to Igor. "To achieve your goal, you need to change your approach. It all starts with adopting a new mindset, the growth mindset. That's how successful people get ahead: by experimenting and taking risks and pushing through their setbacks to learn from mistakes and failure. It is not going to be easy. And I can help you with this."

"But how can I allow myself to make mistakes?" Igor replied." Everything in classical music has to be perfect. And the stakes are so much higher than they were when I was touring with my metal band."

I observed that Igor was in the throes of the fixed mindset: the mindset that is based on the belief that you only have a fixed amount of talent and intelligence and that if you make a mistake, it means you aren't talented. But I could tell that Igor had a great work ethic and wanted to succeed. Moreover, he had signed up for my class, where he would learn how to adopt a growth mindset approach. I explained to Igor that he would be working on a semester-long project that could be a prototype of a music venture and that he would get to explore and experiment with different models. I then told him, "In my class, the only failure is if you quit. I grade on your process and what you learn, not on the end result."

I could tell that Igor was intrigued.

So, Igor began his journey. It was hard at first to let go of the notion that everything had to be perfect. He struggled with his workload, especially since he was taking two business courses at the Yale School of Management and was having trouble keeping up. But then he remembered something else I had told him: that the growth mindset encourages people to reach out and ask for help as a smart strategy for learning. Igor asked a fellow student for help in his accounting class, and slowly, things got a little easier.

Igor initially did not have any ideas for his class project. But he remembered that the growth mindset encouraged going outside your comfort zone to try new things. So he picked up on an idea from a fellow student: how to help musicians get better at their craft. Igor formed a team, and they began working on a web-based portal with videos from professional guitarists showing how to practice effectively. Igor and his team experimented with a few different models. A few times, they hit a wall, but they kept going and completed a successful class project.

The next semester, Igor and a smaller, more targeted team continued to work on the venture. They won a big grant and spent the following summer in a start-up incubator in New Haven learning the business side of creating a successful company called tonebase, with support from mentors and $15,000 in start-up expenses. Igor had discovered his sweet spot.

Igor stopped by my office before graduation in May 2017 to fill me in on his progress. He wasn't going home to Germany to teach guitar. Instead, he was dedicated to making tonebase a success. He told me that he was working harder than ever but was incredibly excited about sharing his vision for tonebase because "nothing felt like failure."

"What's helping you the most, Igor?" I asked him.

Without hesitating, he replied, "The growth mindset that I learned about in class where you are not afraid to experiment and where you learn from failure. This is such a big change from the way I have been approaching my performance career to avoid failure at all costs. These days, I reach out to others if I need help and I learn from my mistakes."

He continued.

"There is no reason to be afraid of failure. Either you win, or you learn. I am now seeing that success is determined by the way you define failure as a learning opportunity. And I am excited about exploring new areas. I feel so much more confident and positive about myself and my company. It does not even feel like I am taking risks!"

Igor and his two partners moved out to California, and later that summer, incorporated tonebase, with Igor as the CEO. Igor had achieved his goal of starting his own music company—just two years after his first meeting with me.

Aftermath

I recently touched base with Igor, who told me that tonebase had just secured its second wave of financing and that the company was expanding rapidly, now adding a piano platform.[1]

The Fixed And The Growth Mindsets

Igor went from confused student to confident CEO in two years and succeeded because he adopted the growth mindset, never giving up, bouncing back from setbacks and challenges, and learning as much as he could.

Dr. Carol Dweck of Stanford University has researched the mindsets of successful people and has developed two different mindsets: the growth mindset and the fixed mindset.[2] Each mindset turns on how you perceive your ability to change how talented and smart you are.

THE FIXED MINDSET

The fixed mindset starts with the belief that you are either born with talent and intelligence or you are not, which means you cannot change how talented or smart you are. The consequence is that you do not want to rock the boat and you are afraid to take risks and make mistakes because mistakes mean you really are not talented. You tend toward perfectionism. You probably play it safe and use the same techniques over and over again, even if you do not see improvement. You are afraid to ask others for help because that is a sign of weakness; asking for help proves that you are not talented or smart.

People with a fixed mindset tend to ride on talent and believe if you are talented, you don't have to exert effort to be good. Moreover, if you have to work hard to get results, it means you lack talent. And if you actually put forth the effort and *don't* succeed, you no longer have any excuses for setbacks, which exposes your lack of talent.[3]

The fixed mindset is tough and extreme, featuring thoughts like:

"I'll never get there."

"I've got to be better than everyone else in order to succeed."

"If only my teammates had been better, we would have performed better. It's their fault that we blew it."

THE GROWTH MINDSET

But there is another approach: the growth mindset.

The growth mindset stems from a belief that you can cultivate your talent and intelligence through hard work, smart strategies, experimentation, and growth. Your talent and intelligence may be the starting point, but success comes as a result of effort, learning, and persistence. You take risks, and when you make mistakes, you learn from those mistakes. You reach out to others for help, and you embrace collaboration. You examine the strategies that work and keep building on them. You discard the strategies that don't work. And you tend to be more resilient and to work harder than people who are locked into the fixed mindset.

It is important to note that the growth mindset is more than simply exerting effort. The growth mindset develops when you use new and smart strategies. The idea is to learn from your mistakes and grow from them, which often involves changing up what you have done in the past if that method has not proved effective.

Whereas the fixed mindset is defensive, the growth mindset means going on the offensive. Students and clients of mine use growth-mindset thoughts like:

"Don't take yourself so seriously. Why not give it a try?"

"No pressure. Just go into it for the experience and see what I can learn."

"This is a process. I can focus and improve."

The growth mindset stems from a belief that you can cultivate your talent and intelligence through hard work, smart strategies, experimentation, and growth.

The fascinating conclusion from Dr. Dweck's research is that people with a fixed mindset are less "successful" than those with a growth mindset approach. People who adopt the growth mindset are motivated by the desire to grow and learn. They are also able to let go of the harsh judgments that characterize the fixed mindset.

Which one are you? To find out, take the mindset quiz on Dr. Dweck's website https://mindsetonline.com/testyourmindset/step1.php.

And the good news is that you can learn how to manage the fixed mindset and adopt a growth mindset approach to your challenges.

How To Adopt A Growth-Mindset Approach

It was the fall of Jennifer's (not her real name)* first year at Yale.

A talented singer with a unique voice, Jennifer enrolled in my class. And while she felt incredibly lucky to be at Yale, she secretly worried that she did not deserve to be there. Just one month into her new semester, she was getting ready to rehearse with a famous conductor in preparation for her first major concert. All she could think about was how she just was "not good enough."

She asked to see me after class one day.

"Professor Baumgardner, as hard as I am working, I am terrified that I will fail at this concert. I am learning so many new things here, and I feel so overwhelmed. I will never be ready in time for the concert," she told me.

"How are you preparing for this concert?" I asked.

"I'm trying to make everything perfect, but nothing is working," said Jennifer.

"You have an excellent work ethic, and you try so hard," I replied. "What can help is to adopt a new approach to the way you work."

"But I've always practiced like this," said Jennifer." I don't know any other way. And I am so afraid to make mistakes because that will mean that I am not really talented."

"I have some ideas on how you can work smarter, not harder," I told her. "Whatever you have done in the past has gotten you to this point

---

* Names followed by an asterisk (*) in this book indicate a pseudonym has been used to protect the creative's confidentiality and privacy.

and now, you need new strategies if you want to reach another level. You need to accept your mistakes as learning tools and find new ways to improve. It will take a lot of work, and it's not an easy path. That's the essence of the growth mindset that you are learning about in class."

"Well," she said, "I want to improve. So how do I do that?"

"Start by embracing the fact that you are having these challenges," I said. "Your job is to tame your fixed mindset. You cannot banish those harsh thoughts that you are a failure. But they are just thoughts, not the truth. You can answer those thoughts and show yourself that you can learn from your mistakes and improve. Then, set some goals that focus on improving, not being perfect. With time, you will begin to see your progress and actually feel that you are growing your talent."

"That sounds really hard," Jennifer said. "But I feel so stressed out these days that I am willing to try."

Jennifer started journaling about her thoughts and saw how pervasive her thoughts of failure were. Then she remembered another thing we talked about: coming up with new, growth-mindset thoughts to override her fears. She wrote down a few helpful ideas, including, "This is only my third week of a new school with a new teacher," and, "I've already improved so much and still have time to work on this duet before the performance."

In addition, Jennifer worked with her teacher to come up with new ways of practicing and performing. She set goals that encouraged her to try out new things, even if they felt risky, and she experimented with new ways of singing. At the first rehearsal, she was very nervous and performed below capacity. But instead of beating herself up, she was able to forgive herself and move on, using her new thoughts to inspire her.

The concert went much better than she expected. It wasn't perfect, but it was a good start. And throughout the year, Jennifer kept working hard and found new ways to improve. She also carefully tracked her mistakes to see what she had learned and also documented her successes to remind herself of her progress. On many occasions, she heard those voices of failure and perfection and sometimes, she gave into them. But she was able to keep going and continue to learn and improve. Through these experiences, she learned to trust herself. As a result, both her confidence and her level of performance grew.

A year later, when the same conductor came back to Yale, she gave a beautiful performance and was the star of the show. Those early fears of not being good enough from the year before gave way to deep satisfaction and confidence.

Tame Your Fixed Mindset With The Four-Step Process

Like Jennifer, you too can tame your fixed-mindset thoughts and adopt a growth-mindset approach using a four-step process.

Step One: Embrace both mindsets.

No one has the growth mindset all the time; we are a mixture of the two.

We all have fixed-mindset thoughts. Some people stay stuck in those thoughts. The successful creative, on the other hand, doesn't stop when her fixed mindset kicks in. Instead, she keeps going.

Dr. Dweck cautions that we cannot banish the fixed mindset. Over the years, many people have labeled the fixed mindset as "bad," and they want to get rid of it. In fact, there is now evidence of what Dr. Dweck calls the "false growth mindset" in those who believe that once they do a little work on their fixed mindsets, they no longer have it. In reality, the two mindsets coexist. Therefore, instead of banishing the fixed mindset, we must learn how to manage it.[4]

Step Two: Understand your fixed-mindset triggers.

Step two is to become aware of what situations trigger your fixed mindset thoughts. Think about the situations in which you hear the voice of your fixed mindset and make a note of what that voice is telling you.

Another way to understand your fixed mindset is to write about what you are like when the fixed mindset takes over. One strategy is to create a fixed-mindset persona that exemplifies what happens to you when you are in the thrall of the fixed mindset.[5] Jennifer's fixed-mindset persona is "Sally," who writes a weekly newsletter, detailing to Jennifer all of her faults. When Jennifer did this exercise in our class, she saw how ridiculous and exaggerated these faults were. It helped her to become more objective about her shortcomings and more determined to address them with a growth-mindset approach.

Step Three: Affirm that you have the power to change.

In step three, you demonstrate your commitment to changing your approach.

You can examine your setback and see what you learned from it. You can weigh the evidence that supports or refutes your fixed-mindset thought. And you can answer that fixed-mindset thought with a growth-mindset thought.

Step Four: Set a growth-mindset goal and take growth-mindset actions.

Now that you have affirmed your power to change, you are ready to take growth-mindset actions.

First, identify the obstacle that is threatening to derail your creativity, like wanting to do everything perfectly or feeling that you are never going to achieve success. Then, set a growth-mindset goal in which you focus on getting better, not being good.[6] You need some gentle and compassionate encouragement to get better at something that is threatening your creative success.

Frame your goal as follows:

By the end of this [quarter/year/season/semester], I want to [improve/get better at/become more proficient in] _____ (be specific so that your growth goal is measurable).

> Then, make a plan and commit to action steps that will help you to achieve your growth-mindset goal. (For details on the four-step process of taming your fixed mindset, see *Creative Success Now: The Workbook*.)

THE POWER OF YET

One last thing: The growth mindset encourages you to see your work as a process. Maybe you have not mastered something *yet*. That one little word can make all of the difference because it overcomes the notion that "I will never get this." In fact, the power of "yet" is the subject of Dr. Dweck's TED Talk.[7]

That's another strategy that helps keep Jennifer going. When she has an off day, she reminds herself that she is not there *yet* and that with hard work, she knows she can improve.

HOW TO ACHIEVE *CREATIVE SUCCESS NOW*

PERSEVERE WITH THE GROWTH MINDSET

1. Track your fixed-mindset thoughts and become aware of the situations that trigger your fixed mindset.

2. Create a fixed-mindset persona to see what you are like when the fixed mindset takes over.

3. Affirm your power to change your approach to a growth-mindset approach.

4. Set a growth goal and make a plan to overcome your fixed-mindset challenge.

5. Stretch yourself and take risks. Fixed-mindset people tend to stick with tasks at which they excel, but eventually, they peak.

6. Reach out to trusted mentors and friends when you are stuck.

7. Adopt new strategies to replace old techniques that no longer work. It's a way to work smarter, not necessarily harder.

8. When working on a challenge, remind yourself that you may not be there yet.

9. Set a growth goal and then make a plan and take action steps that will help you achieve your goal.

CHAPTER FOUR

Get In The Flow With Positivity And Proactivity

 Flow may very well explain why creatives work so hard and persevere through setbacks: because of the incredibly positive feeling of flow when they get it right.

Just ask Jessica,* a choral conductor, who felt on top of the world at a recent performance where she connected effortlessly with the orchestra and the choir and generously shared the beauty of the music with the audience.

Or Chloe,* the head of an opera company, who tapped into her best self when she led a difficult board meeting and achieved consensus on the issues, feeling energized and focused, knowing just what to do without having to think about it.

Or Sam,* a rising executive at a nonprofit, who felt inspiring, energized and as though he were having an out-of-body experience when he delivered a powerful presentation that wowed his audience.

All three of these creatives worked hard to achieve their flawless performances. Their reward was feeling flow: their level of optimal performance. And no wonder, because flow is at the heart of positivity.

Positivity stems from doing things or having experiences that give rise to positive emotions. It's at the heart of positive psychology: the study of human flourishing and what we can do to foster greater happiness in our lives.

In fact, research from positive psychology and neuroscience shows that when you are happy and optimistic and experience positive emotions, you are able to cultivate the kind of mindset and engage in behaviors that give rise to greater success and fulfillment. In other words, success flows from happiness.[7] This research undercuts the notion that you will only be happy when you achieve your success goal, like winning an orchestra job, getting tenure, or making a million dollars.

Moreover, as Dr. Sonja Lyubomirsky demonstrates, 40 percent of your potential to lead a happy life is within your control.[8] You can begin to cultivate happiness by adopting the mindset of positivity through flow (your level of optimal performance) when you voluntarily engage in an activity of intense focus and joy where your skill level meets the challenge at hand.[9]

The Power of Flow

Flow is the brainchild of positive psychologist Mihalyi Csikszentmihalyi. He was fascinated by creative people who were devoted to making their lives worthwhile and meaningful. Csikszentmihalyi researched the conditions that led people to perform at their optimal best and came up with the concept of flow:

You *voluntarily* engage in an *intrinsically* rewarding activity;

You are *focused and clear* on what you are doing;

You have a *goal* and you are getting the *feedback* that tells you how you are doing;

You feel *challenged* and you have the *confidence* that you can reach that challenge;

You feel *inspired* to increase your level of performance and meet the challenge at hand and you are able to do so;

Time goes by and you are so engrossed in what you are doing that you do not even notice; and

You feel *in control* of the experience and believe that you can cultivate and master the skill through training and discipline.[10]

HOW TO ACCESS FLOW

Would you like to access your flow? Here's a quick way to do so.

Recall an experience when you were doing something that you love and performing flawlessly and feeling joyful. This can come from your professional life, your creative output, a leadership experience, a relationship encounter, or any other experience during which you were at your best.

In this experience, you felt challenged yet confident of meeting that challenge. You were totally immersed in this activity and so absorbed in the moment that you didn't even notice the passage of time. And you were doing this just because you loved it.

How did you feel in this experience? Chances are you experienced flow and felt a host of positive emotions. To capture those feelings, come up with a few words that describe what you were like when you were in this wonderful state of optimal performance.

Jessica's flow words were *connected, effortless*, and *generous*. Chloe's were *energized, focused*, and *intuitive*. For Sam, his words were *inspiring, energized*, and *having an out-of-body experience*.

Other flow words that my students and clients have used to describe their experience at flow include *calm, centered, on fire, positive, glowing, floating, invincible* and *powerful*.

What are your flow words?

FLOW AND CONFIDENCE

Flow is a powerful way to inspire your confidence because it is at the heart of positivity. Just ask Barbara Lynne Jamison.

Barbara Lynne, a warm-hearted, generous arts administrator, is passionate about engaging with communities through the arts. She discovered the positive power of flow when she met me at Opera

America's Leadership Intensive, a program designed to identify and bolster the careers of the most promising young opera leaders.[11]

At the time that we met, Barbara Lynne was working in the education department of Seattle Opera after a career as a professional singer. She did not necessarily aspire to take on the leadership of an opera company and was not sure of her career path.

I run the personal leadership component of Leadership Intensive and teach participants how to access and leverage the *Creative Success Now* mindset, including flow. As I explained flow to the Leadership Intensive participants, Barbara Lynne was inspired by the idea of tapping into her level of optimal performance.

"This is amazing," she told me. "Flow is helping me to discover my sources of joy and to tap into my strengths." With the boost of confidence from flow, she committed to exploring the best way for her to serve in the opera world.

Soon after she returned to Seattle Opera after Leadership Intensive, Barbara Lynne was promoted to join the senior management team and run the company's Programs and Partnerships Department.

Slowly, she felt empowered to step into her power and grow as a leader. Using flow helped her to claim that power. The more she engaged in flow activities, the more she stretched herself to grow and improve. Barbara Lynne flourished in her new role.

She created new programming that successfully expanded the reach of the opera company to 70,000 people per year. As a result, the company was able to provide access to audiences and communities who were not typically served by opera—a major goal for today's arts institutions.

She also found another way to use flow in her leadership role: to understand the strengths of the brilliant people with whom she worked and fill out her teams with people who excelled in areas that were not her strengths (more on strengths in chapter 5). Barbara Lynne realized that she was ready to take on the role of leading an opera company. A short time later, after a national search, she became the general director of Kentucky Opera.[12]

As Barbara Lynne discovered, flow is a powerful way to inspire your positivity.

BOTTOM LINE ON FLOW

Flow makes you feel great. When you engage in flow, you experience greater self-esteem and feel more confident.

Flow is a growth experience because the more you engage in flow, the more you stretch yourself and become better at what you do. This helps you to take risks and expand your capacity for courage.

Flow is inherently pleasurable, so you enjoy the process; the ultimate goal is a by-product. As such, engaging in flow activities motivates you to create your success. No wonder people at flow perform flawlessly and passionately—and so can you.

For a more detailed description of how you can incorporate flow into your life, see *Creative Success Now: The Workbook.*

Create Opportunities With The Proactive Mindset

Everyone loves Amy Gewirtz, a lawyer-turned-theater producer, investor, and cofounder of a not-for-profit theater.

Amy was the creator and director of a terrific transition program at Pace University School of Law: New Directions for Attorneys. The program provided guidance, inspiration, and practical skills to attorneys who had left the law and were seeking to transition back to the professional world. Amy was well-versed in career transitions. She had started her legal career as an entertainment lawyer but grew tired of the practice of law. She then shifted her career focus and went to work at her law school alma mater, first in the career office and next in the admissions office. After ten years, she seized on the opportunity to join the career office at Pace University's Law School, where she created the New Directions program with a few colleagues and became its director two years later.

I met Amy when I was invited to speak at the New Directions Program. For four years, twice a year, I lectured on the topic of "Finding Your Passion and Purpose." Amy would sit in the back of the room during these sessions. I often wondered what she was thinking. Then, after my last talk, she told me, "For all these years, I have been listening to you talk about passions, and I have decided that the time has come for me to leave this program and return to my first passion of the theater."

And she gave me a hug.

Amy was thrilled to have created a successful program at Pace and to have helped so many attorneys move toward their next career chapters. After eight years in this role, however, she realized that she was starting to feel a yearning to return to a passion for theater that had been dormant for many years. Now the question was what to do with that passion.

Amy is a doer. And she is not afraid to try things out and see where they lead. After much reflection, she decided to leave Pace and go out in search of her next venture. For six months, she remained as director of the New Directions program and simultaneously began taking classes in commercial theater producing. Not only did she learn the ins and out of being a producer, but she also met amazing theater people. Together with a woman whom she met in one of her classes, they have formed a not-for-profit theater company, Liquid Theatre Collective, Inc., whose mission is to nurture and develop projects with a social-justice or humanitarian component.[13] As executive director of that company, Amy is proud to be developing new work for the theater—all of which was fueled by her early passion, her desire to explore her possibilities, and her ability to make things happen.

This is proactivity, the fourth element of the entrepreneurial mindset: looking for opportunities to create your vision of success and taking action to make that vision a reality. The proactive mindset means that you look for ways to influence your environment and situation.

The proactive mindset means that you look for ways to influence your environment and situation.

Being proactive means that you don't wait for the phone to ring; instead, you initiate those calls.

Take Pulitzer-Prize-winning composer David Lang, Julia Wolfe, winner of the MacArthur "Genius" Grant, and Michael Gordon who met as doctoral students in composition at the Yale School of Music, and together founded Bang on a Can.[14]

When these composers graduated from Yale, the composition world in New York was divided between the "uptown" or academic school of composition and the "downtown" or experimental school whose work was performed in venues like BAM, The Kitchen and The Knitting Factory.

These three composers wanted to erase the lines between the two camps. Together, they founded Bang on a Can with a mission of creating an international community dedicated to innovative music, no matter where it is found. As an experiment, they hosted the Bang on a Can marathon in a small art gallery in downtown New York in 1987. And their experiment paid off. The event was wildly successful, becoming an annual event on the New York cultural scene.

The founders' dream was to create a touring ensemble, start a summer festival, and create a label. A famous arts consultant told them that this was impossible. But this did not deter our three idealistic composers.

As the annual marathon grew in popularity, people from other parts of the United States wanted to experience this new form of music. So, a few of the star performers hit the road to take Bang on a Can to the rest of the US. A new touring ensemble—the Bang on a Can All-Stars—was born.

The three founders also wanted a way to train young musicians in their style of composing and performing. And so, they founded a summer festival at Massachusetts Museum of Contemporary Art fondly known as Banglewood. With all the great music that Bang on a Can was nurturing, the founders then set their sights on creating a new record label, and Cantaloupe Records was born.

Today, Bang on a Can performs and tours widely. The marathon is an annual event. Banglewood is going strong, as is the Cantaloupe record label. All of this was made possible because the founders persevered and proactively went about making their dream a reality.[15]

HOW TO ACHIEVE *CREATIVE SUCCESS NOW*

GET IN THE FLOW WITH POSITIVITY AND PROACTIVITY

1. Recall an experience of flow and embrace the feeling of positivity.

2. Describe what you are like at flow.

3. Take three to five flow words and create your flow affirmation to remind you of what you are like at your best.

4. Tap into your flow self to exude confidence in your creative work.

5. Be proactive by taking action steps toward your dream goal.

6. Spot and create opportunities to make your creative dreams a reality.

7. Experiment and explore new and different fields to generate new possibilities.

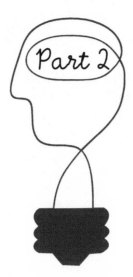

The *Creative Success Now* Authenticity Set

As a creative, you no doubt pour yourself into your work. The more you align your creative work with who you are, the more inspired you will be to work toward your creative success. And it is important to find that inner motivation in order to keep going every day and put your creative work out there.

That's why it's important to discover who you are at your core. What helps is having a profile of yourself at your authentic best, with these three elements:

- Do what you love: your passions.

- Do what you are good at: your strengths.

- Do what is important to you: your values.

What's more, once you identify these three elements, you can articulate your life purpose: your unique way of contributing your passions, strengths, and values to serve the world and make it a better place.

So, let's dive into chapters five and six of the *Creative Success Now* Methodology to define the authentic you.

CHAPTER FIVE

Play To Your Passions And Strengths

The year was 2012, and the place was my coaching office on the Upper West Side of Manhattan. That's when and where I met Anna Friedberg.

Anna, a gregarious lawyer with a wide circle of friends, had just started her first job at a large New York law firm. This was at a time when the recession had dramatically cut the demand for legal services, and law firms had hired too many young associates. Anna had only billed seventy hours in the last six months, whereas the firm's expectation was *200 hours a month*.

She was in danger of losing her job and was really stressed. Plus, she lacked confidence in her legal skills and did not know if she was up to the task. But Anna had just come from a clerkship with a prestigious federal judge. She was great at and passionate about cultivating and managing relationships and creatively solving problems. She also loved to make things happen. As scared as she was, she was determined to come out on top.

That's when she walked into my office. I asked Anna to define what success would look like. "I want to start my own business where I can manage people and solve big problems," Anna said.

"What are you passionate about?" I then asked her.

"That's a hard question," she replied." I can wrap my brain around pretty much any subject, so I don't think I have a passion."

"Let's explore a few more ways to define passion." I replied." What excites you about your work?

Anna thought for a moment and said, "I love to nurture meaningful relationships. I love solving hard problems and coming up with creative, out-of-the-box solutions. I get really excited when I am managing people around a project in order to come up with the best result."

"Here's what we can do to sort out your career challenge," I observed. "You need to build up your confidence and focus on what you are really good at. You need to find ways to use your passion for people and creative problem-solving. Then, we need to find the best match between your strengths and your ideal job. In the meantime, let's work on how you can make the most of your experience at the law firm."

It wasn't easy for Anna. The monthly billing requirement in a slow economy meant that there was not a lot of work at the firm. The threat of losing her job weighed on her heavily.

At first, her hours did not increase. But Anna put her people skills to work and reached out to more senior lawyers in her firm to let them know that she was available to work on their cases. Since she was so likable and reliable, she began to get more work. She dove into her work and did a great job. As her work increased, so did her hours—and so did her confidence.

She also was on the lookout for cases that matched her problem-solving and people skills, as well as her commitment to being of service. Then she learned that the firm had taken on a big *pro bono* case challenging violence at the notorious prison, Rikers Island—the world's largest jail complex. This was the ideal match for Anna.

There were multiple parties involved in the case, represented by a host of lawyers. Moreover, the case presented a complex series of challenges on issues that really mattered to Anna. And there were no easy answers. Anna was thrilled. This was her opportunity to put her passions and strengths to use.

Anna dug in and cultivated excellent relationships with the lawyers and their clients. She worked hard to come up with creative solutions to the many challenges of the case. And she ended up being the point person to organize the case and manage the work so that everyone had a meaningful role to play.

Her breakthrough opportunity came when the case was settled. The case was put under the supervision of a federal monitor whose role was to oversee the settlement and make sure that the parties complied with the terms of the settlement agreement. And guess who was appointed Deputy Monitor?

Anna.

It was not possible to do this work at a law firm, so Anna took her business to a consulting company. It was great to have the security of the company as she made the move from law firm life into the business world. Anna immediately got to work and hired a team. They did a great job for their client, and Anna felt an enormous sense of accomplishment. But Anna was frustrated by the management at her consulting company, which was holding her back. She realized that it was time to start her own venture and run her business independently. It was a big move, but Anna was really good at making things happen and communicating her vision to others. So Anna made a decision to leave the company and start her own firm, named Tillid, taking her existing team with her.[1]

Today, Tillid is a success, and Anna relishes her role as a business owner, managing not only her team but also her complex array of clients, creatively working on the solution to a critical social problem and making the world a better place.

What helped Anna? Playing to her passions for people and complex problem-solving and her strengths as a communicator, relationship-builder, and a person who makes things happen. That's what gave her the boost of confidence she needed to up her profile at her law firm, go after the right kind of work, and then leave the security of a law firm and a consulting company to start and run her own business.

Passion Fuels Creatives

Every creative with whom I work has passion. This is not surprising, for creatives are fueled by their passion: the energy, drive, enthusiasm, and sheer love for what they do. Creativity researcher and Harvard Business School professor Teresa Amabile and leadership professor Colin Fisher observe that this passion drives creative people to pursue their work and become intrinsically motivated to create.[2] Tapping into that passion can inspire you to take that journey toward success and inspire others to join you on that journey.

Most creatives know what their passion is. But sometimes, especially when you are at a point in your career when you are not sure what to do with your creativity, you may wonder if you even have a passion.

What if you don't know what your passion is? No problem. Just like Anna, you may need a broader and more expansive definition of a passion. You can discover your passion in a variety of different ways by exploring:

- The subjects that fascinate you

- Your sense of mission

- The way you interact with people

- Your way of thinking

- Your process for solving problems

Passion drives creative people to pursue their work and become intrinsically motivated to create

TAP INTO YOUR PASSION

To understand the source of your passion, go back to the first time you realized that your creative pursuit was different from everything else in your life. This may come from childhood or any other point in your life when the passion for creating became the driving force of your life.

Go back to the first time that you realized that music or writing or performing or engaging in your creative pursuit was special.

What was that moment? How old were you? Where were you? What were you listening to? What did you see? What did you experience? What was different about your creative passion from anything else in your life?

Take some time to explore where your passion came from. And then you can share this experience whenever you want to inspire the world around you.

Play To Your Strengths

As Anna learned, another key element of creative success is discovering and learning to play to your strengths.

Strengths are natural gifts that you productively apply to maximize your talent. The study of strengths is a major component of positive psychology, with many years of research showing that identifying and using your strengths enhances your capacity for greater well-being and happiness.[3] For starters, studies show you are more likely to reach your goals and be successful if you are doing things that you are good at. It's much easier to play to your strengths than to compensate for weaknesses. The more you develop your natural talents, the stronger they become. And the more you use your strengths and play to your strengths in your personal and professional endeavors, the less of a struggle you will have. When you know and develop your natural talents, the effort you put into a project using a natural strength is much more effective and less work for you than if you are struggling with something that does not come easily to you.[4]

Psychologists Robert Biswas-Diener and Todd Kashan specialize in strengths research and have found that our greatest successes occur when we use and develop our strengths.[5] Moreover, people who have the opportunity to exercise strengths on a daily basis are more engaged in their work and have higher levels of happiness and lower rates of depression.[6]

Moreover, knowing your strengths can help guide your career choices and lead you down a more satisfying career path. As Anna discovered, knowing her strengths helped her pivot to a career that utilizes her top strengths.

And by knowing, using, and playing to your strengths, the more positive and confident you can be with the mindset that is at the heart of fueling your inner motivation to help you to achieve the success that you are looking for.

Finally, focusing on strengths enables you to have more fun at work and work smarter, not harder. This is especially important when working with a team. Julie,* an innovative graphic designer, is a strategic thinker who loves to craft beautiful designs with particular attention to detail. She is also skilled at making business pitches and cultivating great relationships with her clients. However, as a solo designer, she was frustrated because it took her a long time to generate designs and she was often behind in her deadlines.

In the course of her work, Julie began working with another independent designer, Sue.* Julie enjoyed working with Sue who was great at making quick decisions and turning her design concepts around efficiently. Yet Sue was frustrated because she needed help developing new business and wanted to expand her work.

The two decided to combine forces and became partners in a new multidisciplinary design studio. Thanks to their complementary skills

People who have the opportunity to exercise strengths on a daily basis are more engaged in their work and have higher levels of happiness and lower rates of depression.

and strengths, they are able to allocate their work more effectively to allow each partner to play to her strengths. As a result, they were able to develop a more streamlined and cost-effective process. They are also better able to communicate the value of their work and charge higher rates, leading to a more sustainable business.

In short, successful people know what they are good at. They also know what they are *not* good at, so that they can build effective teams to whom they delegate the responsibility for areas in which the team members can shine. And they also know their weaknesses. We will address those a bit later.

This overcomes two big misconceptions:

- You have to be good at everything.

- You need to work on your weaknesses in order to succeed.

That's why it is so important to know and play to your strengths.

DISCOVER YOUR STRENGTHS

Strength work starts with knowing your strengths. There are a few ways to discover your strengths.

FLOW

One way is to go back to the flow experiences you tapped into in chapter 4. Since flow is when you are at the top of your game, you are undoubtedly using your strengths to achieve that level of optimal performance. So, think about what strengths you use while experiencing flow.

COMPLIMENTS

Next, think about what your best friend/significant other says about you. Similarly, reflect on the best professional feedback that you have received.

When people compliment you on a strength, they see something that stands out. They may even notice characteristics of which you may not even be aware. Great bosses and mentors often recognize our strengths. So do our loved ones.

STRENGTHSFINDER 2.0 ASSESSMENT

Yet another way to find strengths is to take a strengths assessment. A good choice is the StrengthsFinder 2.0 Assessment.[7] This assessment was developed by psychologist Donald O. Clifton, founder of the predecessor to the Gallup Organization. Over the years, it has been used by hundreds of thousands of people to help them discover and play to their strengths. The assessment lays out thirty-four strength themes that are divided into four domains of leadership:

- **Executing strengths:** People with executing strengths get things done. They focus, are disciplined, commit to achieving on a daily basis, and/or solve problems to get to a practical solution. You can rely on this person to take an idea and make it happen.

- **Influencing strengths:** Those with influencing strengths take command, initiate projects, and get people on board with their ideas. They communicate powerfully and/or win others over. This is the person who is gifted in persuading others to get on board with an idea.

- **Relationship-building strengths:** People who are strong in relationship building have empathy, create harmony, inspire others with positivity and know how to connect successfully with others. Those with strengths in this domain lead with the ability to understand others and make them feel valued.

- **Strategic thinking strengths:** Strategic thinking strengths involve how you think and learn. This extends to strategic and analytical thinking, generating new ideas, collecting ideas, and having an aptitude for learning. People who are strong in this area lead with their ideas to help make better decisions.

To take the assessment, buy the book, *StrengthsFinder 2.0* by Tom Rath.[8] Then, go online to take the assessment, which takes twenty-five minutes and gives you your top five strengths.

Even if you do not take the assessment, you can use the Strengths-Finder principles to determine which of the four domains of strengths you fall into. Think about what you do best and what energizes you. Then, plot those strengths into one or more of the four domains of leadership.

Put Your Strengths To Work

Now that you know your strengths, let's put them to work for you.

EMBRACE YOUR STRENGTHS

For starters, embrace your strengths. The research shows that you can be successful no matter what strengths you have.[9] Rather than worrying that you don't have strengths in a particular area, or wishing you had different strengths, focus on and own the strengths that you have to see how they can help you to succeed.

One year, I had two students in my class who had all five of their strengths in the strategic thinking area. Initially, they were both worried that they would never get anything done. Yet, both of them did a beautiful job in my class, including the class project for which they were each responsible. Indeed, both of them found the motivation to get these projects completed because they were so inspired by their ideas.

So, lead with your strengths and become known for what you do well.

USE YOUR STRENGTHS APPROPRIATELY

Using strengths wisely and appropriately is a great way to build confidence. It's a lot like Goldilocks and the Three Bears: not too much, and not too little, but *just right*. Thus, people who do not use their strengths often feel frustrated. Conversely, overusing your strengths can also backfire, like overachieving to the point of burnout, thinking so much that you don't get things done, or seeking harmony and lapsing into people-pleasing. The trick is to find the right balance.

Here are five steps to help you make the most of your strengths:

- **Assess** how well you use your strengths.
- **Develop** your strengths.

- **Appropriately use** your strengths: not too much and not too little.
- **Balance** strengths and weaknesses.
- **Redesign your week** to make the best use of your strengths.

By taking charge of your strengths, you will find that getting things done is a lot easier and more effective. Have fun playing to your strengths. And then, let's move on to the next chapter to learn about values and purpose.

HOW TO ACHIEVE *CREATIVE SUCCESS NOW*

Play To Your Passions And Strengths

1. Tap into your creative passion to remember what got you started on your journey.

2. Use your passion to inspire your creative work and inspire others to follow you.

3. Find your strengths by taking the StrengthsFinder 2.0 assessment and writing down five compliments that people give you.

4. Assess how often and how well you use your strengths.

5. Identify the strengths that you do not use enough and make a plan to use them more often and more effectively.

6. Check the strengths that you overuse and dial them down appropriately.

7. Identify the weaknesses that are holding you back and take actions to improve them.

8. Redesign your week to maximize the use of your strengths.

CHAPTER SIX

Align With Your Values And Purpose

E lvis Presley is credited with saying, "Values are like fingerprints. Nobody's are the same, but you leave 'em over everything that you do."

The notion of values reminds me of Ashley Smith, a brilliant, promising Australian musician who came to study in the United States in the hopes of advancing his career.

With his winning smile and open demeanor, Ashley was a talented and original musician with a desire to do something big and something different. However, to be successful in Australia's music scene, he needed a degree from a prestigious US graduate school, which was going to be a long-shot. Even so, he made some recordings and put together his application materials for Yale and a few other graduate schools. He was thrilled when he was accepted to Yale and headed off to the US.

But studying at a high-powered university far from home was hard for Ashley. He had trouble keeping up and was really stressed out. Things got so bad that he decided to take a year off.

When he returned to Yale a year later, he felt reinvigorated to succeed no matter what. But he was not sure of his career direction so he went along with his teacher's suggestion to pursue the "safe" path of an orchestral career.

The problem was that Ashley, despite being a brilliant performer, was flunking his auditions. The reason? He simply could not motivate himself to prepare for the rigorous audition process.[1]

That's when I met him as a student in my class. He shared with me his career vision and his struggle to win an orchestra job.

"What's important to you in life?" I asked. "Tell me your top values."

"Creativity, self-realization, and lifelong learning," was his immediate response.

"And how does orchestral performing align with those values?" I asked him.

"Not at all," he said. "I love variety and new challenges. I am much more excited about being a soloist and premiering works by today's composers than I am about playing in an orchestra. And I would love to be a professor at a university leading a new music ensemble. No wonder I couldn't play well at my auditions! But how do I create that vision?"

I mapped out a few options for Ashley, and he began to formulate his plan. He was a little nervous because of his recent experiences with the orchestral auditions. But the thought of creating a vision that dovetailed with his top values was very exciting. And Ashley discovered his inner motivation to go out and make that dream happen. He worked with the composers at Yale to premiere new work. He curated concerts, programming the music he loved, and put together ensembles of his friends. His final degree recital, which I attended, was a masterpiece of creativity, involving video projections, costumes for himself and his ensemble members, and an amazing variety of repertoire.

As he approached the end of his master's program, he applied to a few universities in Australia for an advanced degree. And in the mail one day, he got the following letter from the University of Western Australia:

> We would like you to start our school's new music ensemble, teach music, and get your doctorate at our university.

And that's what he did. Today, Dr. Ashley Smith—yes, he got his doctorate—is invigorated by the variety of his career portfolio. He tours around his home country and works with contemporary composers to premiere new work. He teaches at the University of Western Australia, where he has won numerous awards for outstanding teaching and leading his school's new music ensemble. What's more, he now has added orchestral performance to his career portfolio and frequently takes on the role of principal clarinet with the West Australian Symphony Orchestra. And he has added a new element to his life: musician health. With the same passion that he exhibits for music, he has taken up CrossFit in order to improve his own endurance and health; he now enters CrossFit competitions and is developing programs for enhancing endurance, fitness, and mobility to improve the health of musicians.

What gave Ashley the courage to pursue this path? Knowing and aligning with his values.

Why Values Are Important For The Creative Path

Values are your qualities of intrinsic worth and the principles that run your life. Core values help to define who you are and what is truly important to you. To be a successful creative person, it is critical to know your values since so much of your work is wrapped up in expressing what is important to you. As Eric, one of my former Yale students, remarked, "Art is such a mess because it's both a job and

Values are your qualities of intrinsic worth and the principles that run your life. Core values help to define who you are and what is truly important to you.

something very personal. Values are a big part of the puzzle." Knowing your values can help you to sort through the "mess" and come up with your own personal code of values, which can help you to pursue a path that feels right.

So, let's sort out the "mess" and explore how to find your personal set of values to form the code of principles that runs your life.

Knowing your values can provide direction in your career and your personal life, help you make important decisions and enable you to feel more engaged in your work. The flip side is that if you compromise your core values, you are likely to experience inner imbalance and stress, just as Ashley did when he was auditioning for orchestra jobs.

When you align your life with your values, you can cut through the swirl of confusion and make decisions that feel right to you. You feel happier. You save time because you don't worry as much or second-guess yourself.

For example, many creatives I know place a high value on their artistic freedom and autonomy.

Take Amanda,* a freelance musician who enjoys a diverse performing career in New York City. As a freelancer, she had the freedom of playing with different ensembles. She consulted me, however, because she wanted even more autonomy by doing more solo performing and having her own business as a film composer and editor. Fast forward a few years, and she has been writing music for commercials while also expanding her solo career.

FIND YOUR VALUES

There are a few ways to find your values.

Reflect on your decision to pursue a creative career and highlight what feels important about that decision. Your values that influenced that decision could be anything from creativity to expertise to relationships.

You can also call up your experience of flow from chapter 4, in which you felt a lot of joy. Often, flow means you are doing something that feels important to you and reflects your values.

On the other end of the spectrum, another approach is to examine stories of anger and frustration, when you felt that someone had violated one of your top values.

BONUS: To help you find your values, download
my Values Assessment from my website at
creativesuccessnow.com/ValuesAssessment.

Now that you know your values, it's time to see how to align your
creative life with those values.

ARTICULATE YOUR VALUES PRINCIPLES

You can take your values off the page and make them a vital part of
your life. Use this three-step process:

- **Step One:** Define your top values.

- **Step Two:** Articulate the principle behind your value.

- **Step Three:** Take an action based on that principle.

Here is how one musician uses these three steps to create his
principles and align his life with his value of lifelong learning.

Step One (definition). I continuously look for new ways to be
creative and to have a variety of platforms for my creativity so that I
am learning and growing all the time.

Step Two (principle). I stand for variety in my creative and
personal life, and I seek out opportunities to perform in different ways;
expand my knowledge base by learning new instruments; collaborating,
commissioning and performing new work; and finding new ways to
share my knowledge through teaching.

Step Three (action steps). There are three action steps:

1. *Program a concert* for the new music ensemble at my university
   where I can showcase a variety of new works.

2. *Organize my summer touring schedule* with a mix of concerts in
   different types of venues where I can play different instruments
   and premiere at least one piece.

3. *Commission an orchestral work* for one composer for the upcoming
   concert season.

So, find your values and articulate your values principles to bring your life into alignment with the things that matter most to you.

Uncover Your Purpose

Kurt Howard was frustrated. A creative, empathetic opera producer, he had moved to New York to take on a high-level executive position as managing director of Opera America, reporting to the CEO. This was the capstone of a rich, twenty-year career, and he considered it his final work position. But although he felt he was meeting the position's expectations, he was not thriving. Something was missing—and he did not know what that something was. He tendered his resignation without having another job lined up and explored a variety of different options in the for-profit business world. In the meantime, Opera America, realizing how valuable Kurt was to the company, split his old job in two and asked him to stay on as director of programming, still reporting to the CEO. This was a much better fit for him, and he felt more connected in his new role, but still wondered what else was possible for him.

That's when we met. It was my third year teaching in Opera America's Leadership Intensive Program for mid-career opera managers, and Kurt was my partner in developing the program. As part of my segment on personal leadership, I had all the participants do a number of assessments, including a Life Purpose Statement. Kurt also also did these assignments and exercises, zeroing in on the Life Purpose Statement.

"What exactly is a Life Purpose Statement?" he asked, as we were getting ready for the first session of the program.

"Your purpose is what gets you out of bed every day." I replied. "It's what connects you to the people you want to serve and how you make the world a better place. And your life purpose statement articulates what your purpose is."

Kurt was curious and wanted to create his own Life Purpose Statement. I laid out the process to him, explaining that it would take some introspection and some hard work.

"You are a committed learner, so I know you can do this," I told him. "Start by coming up with seven experiences in your life where you have felt the most fulfilled."

"I'm not sure I have seven really great stories in my professional life," he commented.

"Actually," I responded, "your purpose is a through line in all areas of your life. Be sure to look beyond your professional roles and also consider your personal life, your community service, your relationships, and even momentary experiences in which you did something wonderful for other people."

"That makes more sense," he replied.

Kurt wrote up seven stories that had touched his professional career as well as successes that had enriched him as a person. We continued the process. I asked him to look for the common threads of how he was using his strengths, passions, and values. And finally, I asked him to consider how he was contributing his talents to serve the world and what impact he wanted to have on others.

Together, we came up with the following statement of purpose:

> *The purpose of my life is to intuitively and confidently inspire, shepherd, and hold up a mirror for self-recognition in myself and others in order to foster contented and related tribes.*

Suddenly, Kurt realized why he had been so stuck. "I have always viewed my role as that of an advisor or the second-in-command," he told me. "But now, I am able to rethink my strengths and see myself as a shepherd, guiding others for a greater purpose than just the transactional nature of the individual relationships."

Once Kurt articulated his purpose, he took a closer look at his life. As much as he enjoyed his job at Opera America, it demanded a lot. Life in New York City was becoming too overwhelming. His personal relationship was suffering. As he read his Life Purpose Statement, he became determined to find a personally joyful lifestyle that incorporated his professional life with other values involving family and service to his community.

And so, even though he had taken the Opera America job thinking that it was his finale, he made the hard decision to move on. Thanks to his network and his excellent reputation in the field, Kurt found a new job at Opera Omaha, where he is shepherding a new community to unlock its creativity and build empathy through the arts.

THE POWER OF PURPOSE

Why do you do what you do?

When I pose this question to creatives, the first answer is often something like:

- To express myself

- To make beautiful music

- To unearth powerful emotional content

And then I probe to find out why expressing oneself, or making beautiful music, or unearthing powerful emotional content, is important to them. That's when they are able to go deeper:

- To inspire audiences with the emotional power of music and create community by connecting one human soul to another

- To improve the human condition and make the world a better place by offering great music

- To unite, uplift, and educate the world around me and spread joy

Welcome to your purpose.

Purpose is how you contribute your best qualities to connect with the audience you most care about and serve the world to make it a better place. It is the intersection of your passions and interests, your strengths and talents and your way of serving others.[2]

WHY CREATIVES NEED TO KNOW THEIR PURPOSE

No matter where you are in your creative journey, knowing your life purpose can help guide you through unknown territory. Knowing your purpose has many advantages:

- It is a practical application of your passions and values.

> Purpose is how you contribute your best qualities to connect with the audience you most care about and serve the world to make it a better place. It is the intersection of your passions and interests, your strengths and talents and your way of serving others.

- It helps you frame inspirational and meaningful goals.

- It inspires you to pursue your vision with confidence.

- It provides intrinsic motivation to pursue what you want to accomplish.

- It provides a roadmap for your future.

- It helps you filter what to say yes to in life and what to turn down.

Moreover, knowing your life purpose provides intrinsic motivation to do your best work because you see your work as a *calling*—where you serve the world and feel deeply aligned with what you do, as opposed to a job—where your paycheck is your main motivator, or a career—where you seek external validation from your title or salary.[3] And perceiving your work as a calling can help you to find greater meaning and satisfaction in your life and work according to the research by Yale School of Management professor Amy Wrzesniewski.[4]

HOW TO CREATE A LIFE PURPOSE STATEMENT

A Life Purpose Statement is your compass to navigate your way through your creative life. It provides clarity around what you want to achieve, a sense of direction on where to start, and the motivation to make it happen. It also can inspire you to greater heights.

To create your Life Purpose Statement, use this four-step process to articulate how you put your talents and passions to work in order to make the world a better place.[5]

Step One: Your Seven Stories of Joy and Fulfillment

Think about seven stories of achievement from your life when you were very proud and felt a surge of joy and fulfillment in the process. Be sure to select stories from different aspects of your life, including creative pursuits, professional accomplishments, education, relationships, community service leadership experiences, hobbies and leisure activities. Focus on the positive aspects of the stories and write down what you were doing that made you feel fulfilled, what you learned from this episode, and the positive emotions you experienced in this story.

Step Two: The Perfect World

Draw a picture of your perfect world: a world in which you and the people you care most about would be happy and fulfilled. Consider how this picture aligns with your passions. What are you doing to get closer to creating the perfect world? How are you using your strengths in working toward creating the perfect world? What is the positive impact on the world and how will the world be a better place as a result of these activities?

Step Three: Your Purpose Qualities, Activities, and Impact

Review your stories to find common themes and words.

- **Purpose qualities:** Consider the strengths and talents that you use to be on purpose.

- **Purpose activities:** Notice what you do to be on purpose and how you are using your strengths and talents to serve your purpose.

- **Purpose impact:** Reflect on the positive impact you are having on the world when you use your purpose qualities and engage in your purpose activities.

Step Four: Your Life Purpose Statement

Then, use the following template to articulate your Life Purpose Statement:

The purpose of my life is to

_____

(What I do to be on purpose)

_____

(My being and/or the qualities I bring to my purpose activities)

so that/in order to_____.
(the impact or the outcome of when I am being and doing on purpose)

Be sure that your statement is sufficiently broad to encompass an expansive vision of your activities and is not limited to what you are doing today.

BONUS: Download the Life Purpose Statement
worksheet from my website at
creativesuccessnow.com/LifePurposeStatement.

Here are some examples of Life Purpose Statements:

From an arts educator: *The purpose of my life is to selflessly, genuinely and honestly create spaces of open-mindedness and empathy in our culture to promote happiness, freedom, and respect for all.*

From a musician who champions diversity: *The purpose of my life is to powerfully and creatively uplift others so that we express ourselves freely and create a diverse and just society.*

From a theatrical projection designer: *The purpose of my life is to lovingly and collaboratively inspire and empower deep connection in order to forge a positive network and create a wave of transformative change.*

Here is my Life Purpose Statement: *The purpose of my life is to expertly and passionately inspire and empower joy and flow so that we spread creativity and exhilaration throughout the world.*

To craft your Life Purpose Statement, please consult *Creative Success Now: The Workbook.*

HOW TO USE A LIFE PURPOSE STATEMENT

A Life Purpose Statement is not a job description. It is meant to be broad and apply to all areas of your life, not just your creative life. The more clarity you have around your purpose, the more success you will have in channeling your talents to make the world a better place.

Just as Kurt did, your purpose can guide you as you assess your current life:

- What are you currently doing that serves your purpose?

- What opportunities can you pursue to help you live your purpose?

- What areas might you explore that align with your purpose?

- How can you say no to things that fall outside your purpose?

By filtering your life decisions through the lens of purpose, you are able to feel more in charge of your life and experience the fulfillment that comes along with knowing that you are doing what you are meant to do.

Finally, if you are not sure of your path, a Life Purpose Statement can help guide you through an exploration goal (more on exploration goals in our next chapter). And as you explore, your Life Purpose Statement can inspire you to go out into the world and have the kinds of fulfilling experiences that can tell you where and how you are serving your purpose.

HOW TO ACHIEVE *CREATIVE SUCCESS NOW*

ALIGN WITH YOUR VALUES AND YOUR PURPOSE

1. Identify your five top core values.

2. Create your Values Principles.

3. Review your major life decisions to see how well they align with your top values.

4. Redesign your schedule to prioritize your values.

5. When you have a decision to make, see how this decision aligns with your top values. If the decision does not feel quite right, consider what values you may have been ignoring.

6. Write up your seven stories of joy and fulfillment.

7. Imagine your perfect world and how you channel your passions and your best qualities into making the world a better place.

8. Create your Life Purpose Statement.

9. Assess how well your current life is in alignment with your life purpose.

10. Filter your decisions through the lens of your Life Purpose Statement.

11. Engage with the world so that your purpose can find you.

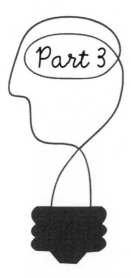

The *Creative Success Now* Skill Sets

Now that you have the right mindset and are clear on your passions, strengths, values, and purpose, it's time to master some essential skills to help you pivot toward creative success. The good news about skills is that they are traits which you can develop with hard work and good strategies, as opposed to inborn talents. Chapters seven through twelve lay out the strategies for acquiring the skills you need to build toward creative success:

- Creative goal-setting and achievement

- Overcoming creativity killers

- Time management for creatives

- Personal branding

- Networking

- Sustaining creative success with financial planning and a good support team

CHAPTER SEVEN

Set And Achieve Your Creative Career Goals

Creatives can be amazingly courageous, especially when the path to achieving creative success is messy and nonlinear.

A case in point is Reena Esmail, a brilliant, vivacious Indian American composer with whom I began working when she was in her doctoral program at Yale.

Reena had a vision of writing music that reflected her dual identity. She had impeccable credentials, with degrees in composition from Juilliard and Yale. She had spent a year in India on a Fulbright Scholarship and was pursuing her doctorate in music from Yale. But she was miserable because to realize her vision, she was working in an environment where very few people understood her full musical language. Reena felt utterly alone.

Reena started out composing in the Western classical style. She spent years honing her craft, and yet she felt the constant nagging that she was not honoring her entire self. While living in New York after graduating from Juilliard, she realized that she wanted to figure out what her identity as an Indian woman truly meant to her. To that end, she began to seek out other Indian women, many of them musicians, and came to understand and love the music they made, which was totally different from Western classical music.

When Reena felt that she had reached her upper limit on her own, she applied to Yale for a master's degree in composition and was accepted. It was a wonderful experience, for it was here that her vision came to her, in a class on Indian music. On the first day of that class, she began to sing, and it hit her: Indian music simply had to be a part of her life.

As elated as she was by this vision, Reena was terrified because it meant stepping outside of what she thought was the right path for a composer. But she felt in her bones that she had to go to India, even if it meant straying from that path. She was awarded a Fulbright Scholarship in India, and she spent the year after completing her master's degree in India, immersing herself in Indian music and culture.

Upon returning from India, Reena entered the doctoral program at Yale, and immediately felt the sting of intense reverse culture shock. Whereas during her Fulbright year, she was not a minority—she was simply another Indian woman studying Hindustani music—she returned to an environment which had previously felt like home to her and now felt utterly foreign. She felt her Indian identity slipping away and felt compelled to fit herself into more conventional standards.

To find a supportive community, she joined my coaching groups at Yale, a magical process whereby a small set of peers meet to discuss and strategize about the experience of creating success as musicians and artists in the twenty-first century. I had created the groups in order to provide a positive, supportive, and safe environment in which to share successes and challenges. To promote safety, we agreed that everything shared in the group was confidential.

Reena was the oldest member of the group, the only composer, and the only doctoral student. The other members were all first-year master's students pursuing performance degrees. And because everyone else was in such a different place from her own, Reena felt safe to open up. For their part, the younger members of the group looked up to Reena, who in their eyes was a superstar. The magic of this group was that from the outset, the members felt free to share their vulnerabilities and support each other with great respect and fondness.

Midway through the year, we had a meeting to discuss career goals. As we went around the circle, Reena announced the goal for her Yale doctorate: "To bring together both halves of my musical life, Hindustani and Western classical music." We discussed the goals, and I then asked each person to share what challenges they faced.

When it came time for Reena to share, she opened up. "I don't know if I have what it takes to do this. There are no role models for what I am doing. I feel so alone in this pursuit. I wonder if it's even worthwhile to get my doctorate, and I keep thinking about dropping out of the program."

Instead of judging her, the other members of the group encouraged her to keep going. For my part, I also reminded her to be true to her authentic self and to write the music to which she was committed.

The coaching group became Reena's refuge as she battled through her doctorate. As powerful as her vision was, she questioned whether she was capable of being taken seriously in the compositional world with her unique form of music, even as she had a full season of commissions outside of the school. Though she delivered on what was demanded of her through sheer force of will, she felt so broken that on multiple occasions she considered dropping out of the program. But she was committed to learning all she could from her wonderful and supportive composition teacher, Aaron Kernis. She worked hard to figure out how to move forward in her creative practice while remaining true to her own voice. And by the end of her doctorate program, she had honed her voice and was already experiencing a lot of success.

Reena moved to Los Angeles as a self-supporting composer. In addition to the many commissions she received, she also committed to working with people in lesser-served communities. This dovetailed with another discussion from our coaching group about how the best career choices reflected your values. It dawned on her that her music was intertwined with genuine human interaction and that she needed her music to engage and create meaningful connections with others in lesser-served communities. Reena found her way and became the composer-in-residence to Street Symphony, a nonprofit music organization dedicated to social justice, working with communities experiencing homelessness and incarceration in Los Angeles.[1]

Today, Reena is thriving. She composes full-time and has five years' worth of commissions ahead of her. She is also the founder and Co-Artistic Director of Shastra, an organization that supports musicians who work between the great musical traditions of India and the West.[2] Reena employs a staff of four to help her with the logistics of her career: from commission negotiations and score sales and rentals to copy work, travel booking, invoicing, royalty collection, and web design. Her work is performed throughout the United States and internationally, and she is committed to her mission of "bringing communities together through the creation of equitable musical spaces."[3]

I caught up with Reena recently to congratulate her on all her successes. She is indeed living her dream and ultimately feels that she is serving a greater purpose because "I am creating a community I want to be a part of through the music I write." She stays focused on what is important to her by her commitment to writing music every single day, whether it's twenty minutes or several hours, always checking in with her long-term vision, consulting her mission statement once a week, and having very-short-term goals to keep her on task.

What helped Reena to push through her doubts and create her success? Allowing herself the freedom to explore and develop her authentic voice as a composer, believing in her vision even when she did not see it reflected in her surroundings, and working tirelessly to make her vision a reality with her short-term goals.

Creativity is messy, and goals can help to channel the creative drive in order to achieve great things. The more you allow your vision and goals to reflect your authentic self, the more inspired you will be to overcome your challenges and achieve what you long to see in the world.

Why Creatives Need Goals

Success in the creative world is far from linear. What helps is to set goals to channel the messiness of creativity and work toward a result you want to achieve in a certain period of time. You need that time period because otherwise, your goal is a mere wish. Goals translate your dreams of creative success into a realistic benchmark and form the basis for your plan to achieve them.

When your goals reflect your passions, strengths, values, and purpose, you feel inspired and intrinsically motivated to frame and pursue your dreams. Those dreams can feel overwhelming, but with a good system, you can articulate an inspiring goal and then break it down into manageable action steps. And the more inspiring your goal, the more motivated you will be to jump over the hurdles that may get in your way. Creative career goals provide a structure to empower you to work toward your success.

Let's tie together your passions, values, strengths, and purpose to create inspiring career goals.

Three Ways To Set Your Big Goals

Creative goal setting starts with a decision: what you want to achieve. This is the place to dream big, because no one is going to dream for you.

That might feel audacious, but it's the way to inspire your creative success. Not sure what that creative goal looks like? Here are three ways to frame your creative goals.

FIRST GOAL-SETTING TECHNIQUE: WHAT'S YOUR BIG DREAM?

Dr. Clayton Shiu, a creative, charismatic doctor of acupuncture, had a vision: to create a style of medicine blending Eastern and Western traditions that would change the American system of health care.

Clay started off life as an academically brilliant and musically talented student. Encouraged to study piano at the prestigious Curtis Institute of Music, he rebelled against his traditional Chinese parents and took up jazz trumpet. His other favorite activities were martial arts—whose rhythm and cadence mirrored what he loved about music—and Chinese medicine, which he learned from his Tai Chi master. These experiences inspired him to pursue medicine and eventually acupuncture since he was passionate about healing patients.

After getting his graduate degree in acupuncture, Clay opened a series of clinics in New York, specializing in sports injuries. Over the course of fifteen years, he took time off to travel the world as an apprentice to a master teacher of Chinese medicine. He combined this knowledge with his clinical skills and observed that his patients were experiencing excellent outcomes. Clay was becoming known as the go-to acupuncture sports injury doctor in New York, and he decided that it was time to focus exclusively on building his acupuncture practice.

Clay then joined the medical practice of a highly respected doctor on Manhattan's Upper East Side, and his reputation as a sports injury specialist exploded. But after a few years, he had plateaued, and he was bored. He realized that it was time to expand his knowledge base. He found his opening by observing that the next frontier in medicine was a better understanding of the brain and that Western medicine did not have all the answers. This was when his vision of creating a new style of medicine came to him. Clay decided to pursue a doctorate of acupuncture with the world's leading stroke rehabilitation acupuncturist, Dr. Shi Xue Min, in Tianjin, China. Over the course of four years, Clay took time away from his acupuncture practice in New York to study in China. Within his first year of working with Dr. Shi Xue Min, he began to integrate what he was learning in China with his twenty years of experience as a practicing acupuncture doctor. Slowly, he developed his own system of acupuncture, which he called Nanopuncture. He was now determined to make his vision a reality.

First, he wanted to make sure that his system worked and that it was reproducible in the United States. To that end, he used his clinical practice to refine his techniques and create a workable system.

Next, if he wanted to change US health care, he needed to teach others how to practice Nanopuncture. After receiving his doctorate from the Chinese university, he began teaching his method, first in

American acupuncture doctoral programs, and then by creating alliances with organizations outside of academia. Through his travels around the US, he was able to identify superstar practitioners around the country. He was now developing an international reputation with his new methods, and his vision was becoming more real. He was beginning to see that it might very well be possible to change health care in America.

Then it hit him: As much as he enjoyed his work at the Upper East Side medical practice, it was time to open his own clinic and train his own team of practitioners. There were a lot of challenges to doing so: Running his own clinic would cost a lot of money since rent in Manhattan is expensive; he had to hire and train a new team and staff and had never done so; and most of all, he had to believe in himself. But he realized that he had learned all that he could from his situation and that the time was right for him to make a change. Clay shared his dream with me one day, and I encouraged him to take the leap of faith.

"You are so passionate about your vision, and you sound ready to take this big step," I told him. "The world needs your ideas, and you are the one to make it happen."

Clay opened the Shiu Clinic in Medical Manhattan earlier this year, integrating neuroscience acupuncture with Western medicine. He has a new team and a new staff delivering the unique Nanopuncture system. His clinic is thriving, and he continues to teach and spread his method around the country.[4]

He recently told me, in his humble fashion, "When you take the big step and acknowledge yourself, you realize that other people have been waiting in the wings for you to do just that."

How did he do this? Clay had a powerful vision of the ideal state that he longed to create. He translated that vision into a series of smaller goals and action steps, overcoming his obstacles with hard work and a belief in himself.

If you have a powerful vision, write it down as your goal, specifying your time period for accomplishing that goal. The decision to make that dream a reality will serve as your magnet to pull you forward as you take the steps toward making your goal happen.

If you do not *yet* have a vision, no worries. Move on to the next technique.

SECOND GOAL-SETTING TECHNIQUE: CREATIVE CAREER OPTIONS

The second way to create your big goal is to consider your options in your creative career and decide which one(s) excite(s) you the most. To do this exercise, use the Creative Career Options Circle.[5]

The Creative Career Options Circle lays out eight broad areas to consider:

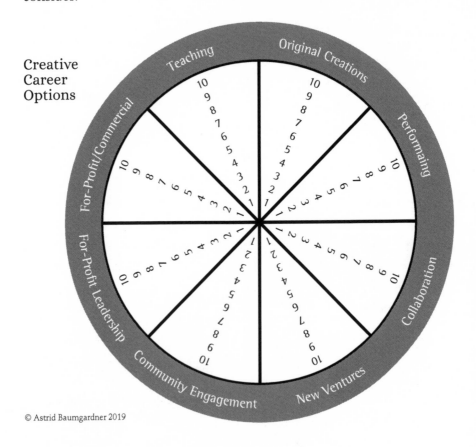

Creative Career Options

© Astrid Baumgardner 2019

Here is how we define each area:

1. **Original Creations:** Composing, writing, choreographing, painting, graphic design, visual art, video games, computer

programming, processes, or anything else that you do to generate a creative product

2. **Performing:** Acting, stand-up comedy, performance art, orchestra, ballet, opera, ensemble, motivational speaking, or any other type of performance before an audience

3. **Collaborations:** Working with creatives in another genre or discipline to generate new work where the sum is greater than its parts

4. **New Ventures:** Creating a new organization, ensemble, business, nonprofit venture, venue, or something else that is new to your creative scene

5. **Community Engagement:** Working as a teaching artist or otherwise bringing your art to a community

6. **Nonprofit Leadership:** Working for or with an existing nonprofit

7. **For-profit/Commercial:** Working for or with an existing business or for-profit arts structure

8. **Teaching:** Teaching either through an institution or with private students

Here's how to set a goal using the Creative Career Options Circle:

Go through each of the eight options and rate how important each option is to you on a scale of 1–10, with 1 meaning "not important" and 10 meaning "can't live without it." This is not a zero-sum game so you can have more than one 10.

Next, go to your highest rated areas. Write down what you would like to achieve in a given period of time. Feel free to combine areas if your goal spans more than one area. Be sure to examine how your goal reflects your values and your strengths.

That's your big goal.

The Creative Career Options Circle helped Russell Fisher, a musician in his master's program at Yale, to zero in on his top goals. He rated teaching as a 10 and easily articulated his goal: to become a university professor at a liberal arts university. His other top areas were performance and collaborations, and he wanted to combine these two areas and fold them into teaching. His big goal thus became to teach at a liberal arts university with ample performance opportunities and collaborations with composers and other artists within five years.

Russell was excited to set this goal because it aligned with his values of knowledge, community, and sense of purpose. And to accomplish this goal, he tapped into his strengths as an achiever and problem-solver, with a shorter-term objective of getting into an excellent doctorate program, which he achieved the following year when he was accepted to the Yale School of Music.

THIRD GOAL-SETTING TECHNIQUE:
SET AN EXPLORATION GOAL

If you are still unsure about your creative success goal, perhaps you are not ready to commit to one goal. Or maybe you have multiple passions and interests, and you cannot decide which one to follow. Or you may simply be afraid to make the wrong choice.

No worries; you are in good company. Like Andrea Kornbluth.

Andrea was a gifted problem solver. Armed with a degree in art history and a knowledge of Japanese, Andrea headed to Japan after college and found a job with a large trading company as the resident problem solver. For fifteen years, she handled the routine day-to-day operations as well as complex, oddball problems ranging from creating their website to negotiating the settlement of an oil spill.

After her Japan sojourn, she returned to America to attend law school, all the while continuing to work for the Japanese company as their US representative. But she ran into a problem she could not solve. None of the career options for law school graduates appealed to her.

To sort out her confusion, she hired a career counselor, hoping that the process would lead to some answers to her career quandary. After undergoing a week-long battery of tests, the career counselor told her, "Sorry, we can't help you. You are just too complicated." And Andrea was back at square one.

But she did not stay there for long.

That's when a frustrated Andrea came to see me. She told me that she had flunked her career tests and asked if I could help her sort out her future.

"You have so much going for you," I began. "What would you like to do?"

"I want a job where I can use my legal training and solve complex problems," she said. "I love my local community and would like to do something to help them. I want to make a difference. And I am worried that I will never figure this out."

"That is going to be a challenge," I told her. "What you need to do is to try out some new areas and see what emerges."

"But I am not sure that there is anything that will let me connect with my creative side, which seems to have fallen by the wayside," said Andrea. At that, she handed me a poster that she had designed. The layout was striking, and the play on words was really funny.

"Very clever!" I remarked. "With all your creativity and your knack for creative problem-solving, let's design some experiments so that you can test out a few new areas and see where they lead you."

"I'm a little nervous after my experience with those career tests," was her reaction. "But I like this new approach, and I am game to try it out."

So Andrea launched a series of experiments. First, she investigated doing work for a small business law firm, but that did not seem to be a good fit. To get back into the creative flow, she took a writing class and started a blog about her local community. She then got involved with a zoning project in her neighborhood. It dawned on her that she loved solving problems for people. Instead of practicing law, what if she became a mediator and consultant?

"But I have no formal training in mediation," she said.

That was remedied when she signed up for a mediation course, at which she excelled.

Andrea began work as a mediator, served on a local community board, consulted with clients including her Japanese company, and continued her blog. And she felt really energized by having a variety of outlets for her strengths and talents.

The aftermath to Andrea's story is that on top of these professional engagements, she has reconnected to her early passion for making art and is now showing her work in various galleries around town and selling prints through her website.[6] As for the process, she discovered it paid off to take actions that are consistent with her character, stay open to new possibilities, and make course corrections along the way. The moral of the story is it is better to experiment than to waste energy worrying.

So, the third way to find your creative path is to set an exploration goal, framed as follows:

For the next _____, I will explore the following areas: _____.

(Time period: Six months, semester, year)

Conducting life experiments to figure out your career path dovetails with the research on successful transitions from Herminia Ibarra, professor at the INSEAD Business School. In her book *Working Identity: Unconventional Strategies for Reinventing Your Career*, Professor Ibarra documents the experience of thirty-nine people who made successful midcareer transitions by experimenting in different areas and discovering a new career path by trial and error.[7]

This method takes a lot of pressure off because you can spend your time learning. If you are worrying about your future, it actually blocks you from the learning process because you are not in the moment. And interestingly, when you relax into your learning, your goals will emerge.

Take a page from Andrea and give yourself some time to find out what you like and where your natural talents lie. Just be sure to give yourself a time period within which to conduct your exploration and keep checking in with yourself on what you are learning.

WRITE DOWN YOUR GOAL

Now that you have a goal, the next step is to write it down. A recent study confirms that people who write down their goals, share the information with a friend, and send weekly updates are 33 percent more likely to achieve their goals than those who do not engage in this process.[8]

Finally, check to make sure that no matter what type of goal you have framed, it reflects your passions, strengths, values, and purpose.

SET AN INTENTION

To supercharge your quest to accomplish your creative goal, set an intention for your dream.

All you do is pick a period of time down the road and state what you are doing in that future time. The trick is to write this in the present tense, as though you are already doing it:

In _____*years, I am a* _____*doing*_____.

Why does setting an intention work? Because if you are able to visualize what you want to do and capture that thought in writing, you are likely to seize the opportunities that will make that dream a reality.

It's fine to write your intention in broad strokes

- In five years, I am a happy and balanced creative person.

- In five years, I am making a living as a creative person.

- In five years, I have a family and a secure creative life.

If you can see it, write it down as if you are already doing it. Then look for ways to make that dream a reality. You will be amazed at the results. Setting your intention is the first step in formulating your Career Success Action Plan.

> Bonus: To help you craft your career plan, download my Creative Career Success Action Plan at creativesuccessnow.com/CreativeCareerSuccessActionPlan.

The *Creative Success Now* Goal Achievement Process

Now that you have a goal, it's time to accomplish that goal. For many people, working to achieve a goal can feel overwhelming. However, the *Creative Success Now* goal achievement process breaks down the process into a series of manageable steps that lead to successful outcomes.

SMART Goals For Smart Creatives

For starters, take your big goal and break it down into manageable pieces that you accomplish in a sequence of shorter-term goals. A helpful strategy is to follow the SMART goal process:

SMART stands for:

- **S**pecific: What specifically do I want to accomplish?

- **M**easurable: How will I know when I reach my goal?

- **A**ttainable: Is it possible for me to reach this goal? (Hint: The answer has to be *yes*.)

- **R**ealistic: How realistic is this goal in the context of my life?

- **T**ime-bound: In what period of time will I accomplish the goal?

The point of SMART goals is to bring the big dream into a time period in which you can see success (T). It requires you to be specific about your big goals (S and M). It makes sure that you believe in your dream (A) since you *must* answer yes to the question, "Is it attainable?" And it has a built-in reality check by asking how realistic the goal is (R).

Without SMART goals, you may be too overwhelmed to pursue your big goal, because once you have your SMART goals, the way forward is much clearer.

Tyler Mashek, a percussionist, learned about SMART goals at the Sō Percussion Summer Institute (SōSI), a summer program at Princeton University founded by the members of Sō Percussion for college percussionists and composers.[9] I met Tyler one summer when I was giving a workshop at SōSI on career planning.

Tyler shared his five-year goal with the group: to work in stage production. But he had no idea how to get there. Using the SMART goal process, he was able to break down his five-year goal as follows:

- Three years: Be an apprentice and freelance in stage production.

- One year: Network and fill in my skill gaps in lighting systems, live sound, and the professional process for how to get things done.

- Three months: Identify the people in the community who might be leads for apprenticeships.

As it turned out, Tyler was able to achieve his three-month SMART goal on the spot because Adam, one of the members of Sō Percussion, who only learned about Tyler's goal at the workshop, told him that Sō Percussion worked with all the best production people in New York. Adam promised to introduce Tyler to the production people right away. In addition, Adam mentioned that Sō was going to tour with a big show in the fall and that the members of the ensemble were planning to do some of the work themselves. Tyler could be that person and immediately gain experience.

The following fall, Tyler got his first gig to join the stage crew of Sō Percussion's touring show. From that experience, Tyler has subsequently gone on to begin a career in stage production, a field he was able to break into by creating SMART goals.

The moral of this story? Not only do SMART goals motivate you to achieve those goals, but also, if you have a dream, tell people about it. You never know what you will find.

LINE UP YOUR ASSETS:
STRENGTHS AND OPPORTUNITIES

To help you achieve your goals, be sure to identify your strengths and opportunities. By identifying your strengths that will help you achieve your goals, you are cultivating the positive mindset because it reminds you of what you are good at.

Successful creatives also know how to spot, create, and leverage opportunities. This is one aspect of the proactive mindset that inspires you to take the initiative as you seek ways to achieve your career goals, rather than waiting for things to drop in your lap.

Composer Missy Mazzoli came right to New York after getting her master's degree at Yale. She was smart, determined, hard-working, and realistic. As a young, unknown composer, she knew that it would be hard to find professional performance opportunities. So, rather than waiting to get performances, she formed her own ensemble, Victoire, to perform her music, with Missy on keyboard. They went on to produce a hit CD. Along with a lot of other hard work and determination, Missy won a lot of commissions and has become a leading voice in contemporary composition.[10] And she is a vital part of a strong and supportive new music community comprised of artists with complementary skills and shared goals.[11]

Scan your world for those opportunities, look for ways to create your own prospects, and start to make things happen.

IDENTIFY YOUR CHALLENGES AND STRATEGIZE HOW TO OVERCOME THEM

Setting goals is not the hard part of goal achievement. Rather, it is persevering toward your goal when challenges arise. And that's where many people stop. Often, these challenges fall into one or more of the following five areas:

- Skills/education

- Professional experience

- Personal development (e.g., time management, lack of confidence, and perfectionism)

- Career advancement (e.g., networking, career planning, and branding)

- Finances

But successful creatives face their challenges. Begin by identifying the area(s) that might be holding you back.

STRATEGIZE

The next step to achieving your goals is to strategize both how to accomplish your SMART goal as well as how to overcome any challenges that may thwart that goal.

Go back to your Creative Career Options Circle and look at your top-rated areas and your goal for that area. Next, rate where you are in the process of achieving that goal. Don't be surprised if there is a large gap between your two ratings. Think about what it would take to increase the gap by one or two points in a specified time period. These actions are the strategies that you can use to work on your goals.

If you have identified the challenges to your goal, give yourself a lot of points, because it takes courage to face your challenges. Once you are able to articulate where you need to improve, you are on the road to solving that problem.

Don't know how to score a piece? Write the first chapter of your novel? Choreograph a new dance move? Here are some strategies:

- Take a class.

- Ask a teacher or mentor for help.

- Shadow an expert for a day.

COMMIT TO YOUR ACTIONS

Now it's time to take those strategies and turn them into action steps with a deadline. I define an action as anything you can put on a to-do list and cross off when you accomplish it. You can frame your action steps by asking yourself, "What is the first step?" or "What is stopping me?" That's your action for the week. Make it a SMART action, with a due date and a specific, measurable result that you can accomplish, framed as follows:

By next Friday, I will:

- Enroll in a class.

- Make a date with my mentor to figure out how to write the first chapter of my novel.

- Email my friend to set a date when I can watch him choreograph a new dance.

And put that SMART action in your calendar so that you will remember to do it.

LEARN AND GROW

As we have seen, achieving those big goals is an iterative process. To keep the learning going, here are a few guidelines.

Keep tabs on your progress: As you work on your goals, see what is working. Each time you reach a SMART goal, write down your process, concentrating on what worked, and use that process the next time you set and achieve a goal.

Make adjustments: When you reach one of your goals, set another. If the goal does not seem to be working, adjust and revise. Learn from your challenges.

Pay attention to what works and what does not: Notice what you like. What you love. What you are good at. What you are not enjoying. It's all good information and can help you to home in on the areas that you want to explore.

Keep a success journal. Document your achievements. And remember that success does not have to be winning the Pulitzer Prize or getting the next promotion. When working on your goals, completing the first draft of your first chapter is a success. Showing your work to a trusted mentor and soliciting feedback is a success. Taking a break to refresh your creative process is a success.

My Goal-Achievement Story

Allow me to share my personal experience with setting and achieving big goals.

When I was in coaching school, I knew that I wanted to help creative people become successful, but I was not sure exactly what that would look like. One evening, I attended a coaching class. The teacher introduced himself as follows.

"Hi. I'm Jim. I'm a lawyer, a coach, and a talent agent. And I teach at the Fashion Institute of Technology."

At that moment, a lightbulb went off in my head, and I realized what I wanted to do. In my journal, I wrote the following goal: *In five years, I am teaching at a major conservatory like Juilliard (or maybe even Yale).*

It felt incredibly powerful and exciting to hit upon my own vision of success. The next day, I woke up and said, "If I am going to achieve this in five years, I need to get started!"

I told my coaching peers about my goal. I designed a few workshops and tested them out on my coaching colleagues, soliciting their valuable feedback. I then reached out to my friends on the Juilliard faculty and offered to come in and teach their students about career success. They were kind enough to invite me in to teach a few classes.

One of my friends on the Juilliard faculty introduced me to the head of Juilliard's career office. She, in turn, hired me to teach a few more workshops. That winter, I gave a series of talks at Juilliard.

By the time the summer rolled around, I had done five full workshops at Juilliard. I knew the deputy dean of the Yale School of Music and approached him to offer to do some career work at Yale. He hired me to give a few guest lectures at Yale and at the Yale School of Music summer program at Norfolk. At Yale, I knew I had found my people. It was the perfect fit. After the summer, I had lunch with the deputy dean, who asked what I wanted from my relationship with Yale. "I want to come to Yale and start your career program and teach your career entrepreneurship track," I told him. That was easy since I had written down my five-year goal in my journal.

"Well," he said, "Your timing is excellent because we have just revised our curriculum and we need someone to head up our new career initiatives." And so, a few months later, after I submitted a few draft syllabi, I was hired to head the Office of Career Strategies at the Yale School of Music and to teach career entrepreneurship, two years ahead of schedule.

Still stuck? Tune into our next chapter.

HOW TO ACHIEVE *CREATIVE SUCCESS NOW*

SET AND ACHIEVE YOUR CREATIVE GOALS

1. Start by creating an inspiring goal—one that you are excited to accomplish by tapping into a vision, using the Creative Career Options Wheel or setting an exploration goal.

2. Break down your goal using the SMART goal process.

3. Line up your strengths and leverage your opportunities to help you achieve your goal.

5. Identify your challenges and strategize how to overcome the challenges.

6. Commit to experimenting when you are not sure of your goal.

7. Take weekly action steps toward your goal.

8. Learn from what is not working, as well as building on what is succeeding.

CHAPTER EIGHT

Overcome The Three Top Creativity Killers

To the rest of the world, Jake,* an engaging, brilliant musician and teacher, looked like a success. The graduate of a major conservatory where he had won all the top prizes, he was on track to get tenure at his university and was an acclaimed performer and the artistic director of his own summer festival. But inside, he was a wreck.

Compelled to do everything perfectly, he could not make time for his project (which had been in the works for over a year) to commission and record new work for his instrument, and he felt creatively stifled. He felt that his level of playing was just not as good as that of his peers. He longed to write a blog but was scared of what others would think. His life partner was so upset at his inability to move forward in his life that she left him.

That's when he reached out to me.

"I am stuck," he told me. "I want to write my blog and release my CD and perform and tour with my friends. But I just don't have the courage to put out my new work. I feel so inadequate compared to my peers. I know that I am not living up to my potential, but I am terrified of making the wrong choices about my future. I am exhausted. I feel like such a failure."

"It sounds as though you are in thrall to your fears," I responded. "You are comparing yourself to others. And I am hearing the voice of perfectionism. The result is that you are not able to do your best work. No wonder you are frustrated and feel like a failure. I can show you some new ways to think about yourself. It will take time for you to adopt a new approach. And it involves a lot of hard work. But I have confidence that you can tackle those thoughts and recharge your creative spirit."

So Jake got to work.

Just sharing his fears with me was a big help. Jake doubled down to see what he could do to move forward. Through coaching, I taught him about the growth mindset and how the best way to move ahead was to try things out and take a few risks.[1] This was a huge shift in his thinking that took some time to sink in. The need to be perfect was hard to overcome and Jake started slowly. He tapped into his values of expertise and realized that he knew more than he thought. That gave him the courage to start his blog.

Using the growth mindset also helped him to reframe his CD project as an experiment. At his summer festival, he found a safe community of trusted friends and colleagues. After a few stumbles, he remembered that performing his new work was an experiment and he had the courage to perform one new piece. His colleagues were most encouraging, and he continued to roll out a few more performances.

Jake is now on track to release his CD. His blog is a hit. He is about to go on tour with his favorite collaborators. And he feels much better about his creative output.

The Three Top Creativity Killers

Being a creative is challenging. You chose this path because of your passion for and commitment to creating something new, different, and better. Yet you are often forging your own path without a clear road map. And sometimes, that path to success and fulfillment seems impossible to achieve and you might be tempted to throw in the towel.

There are always external challenges to creative success: the economy, the competition in your sector, your current level of skill and experience. But by committing to new learning and developing effective strategies, you can probably overcome these challenges.

The real roadblocks to creative success are your inner roadblocks, the creativity killers: fear, perfectionism, and compare-and-despair.

While we cannot control our external circumstances, we can control ourselves. And with the right mindset and some good strategies, you can overcome the internal obstacles that kill creativity and get your creative work out there.

FIRST CREATIVITY KILLER: FEAR

Many high-achieving creatives set very high standards for themselves and consider themselves failures when they fail to meet those standards. They also worry that failing to attain these standards will kill their careers. On top of those fears, many creatives are paralyzed by the fear of making the wrong choice in the face of uncertainty. Not only do these fears impair self-esteem, but they also lead to exhaustion, burnout, and in some cases, abandoning one's creative dreams.

So, what helps to get back on track?

Articulate and Narrow Your Fears

As Jake experienced, talking out and articulating your fears is the start of conquering them. Instead of allowing your fears to rattle around in your head, face them head on and zero in on the true source of the fear.

Examine the Evidence of Failure

These deep-seated fears may *seem* real, but in fact, they are not the truth. We often exaggerate and go to extremes in writing down our fears. What helps is to examine the facts that you think demonstrate that you are a failure and compare them with the objective circumstances showing that you are, in fact, working your way toward success.

For example, Will* made some mistakes in a recent performance and felt that he was such a failure that he would never make it as a musician. As evidence of his "failure," he cited that performance. But to counter his immediate thought, he wrote down the following three things:

"My audiences respond enthusiastically to my performances."

"I feel inspired when I play."

"I am making a lot of progress in my playing."

This helped Will to see that his fear of failure was exaggerated. He then committed to working hard with his new teacher to make even more progress.

Embrace the Growth Mindset

Another way to combat the fear of failure is to learn from your setbacks. Joanne,* a master's student at Yale, has been taking orchestral auditions and has not yet won a job. At the first few auditions, she felt like a failure, which triggered her fixed mindset—the mindset that told her that she was not talented enough to succeed.

But in the spirit of the growth mindset, Joanne did not wallow in self-pity and fear. Instead, she solicited feedback and examined how she could improve her playing. And by learning from her mistakes, she has felt more prepared and more confident and is now getting closer to her goal of an orchestra job.

To quote John Maxwell, "Sometimes you win, and sometimes you learn."[2]

Reframe Your Action Steps As Experiments And Let Go Of The Results

Once Jake was able to reframe his action steps toward his CD project as an experiment, he felt free to explore his possibilities and was able to start performing. And the feedback he received helped to improve the project.

This is another great way to combat the fear of failure with the growth mindset: Set up your actions as part of the learning process so that you can improve. Underlying this mindset is the ability to let go of expectations and to liberate yourself from negative self-judgment. This makes it easier to take on challenges and present yourself at your best.

Practice Success Through Small Victories

It's easy to fall into the trap of defining success as a competition win—and nothing short of a win. So, practice success through small victories: the steps along the way that you have been able to achieve.

This makes it easier to build on the smaller successes as you work your way up to larger accomplishments.

SECOND CREATIVITY KILLER: PERFECTIONISM

No wonder Jake was so exhausted! He strove to make everything he did—from teaching to performing to writing a blog to creating his CD project to writing emails—perfect. And his aspiration to create the perfect CD project and the perfect blog pretty much stopped him in his tracks.

Meet one of the top creativity killers: perfectionism—the voice of your inner critic. It takes a lot of courage to put your creative work out there. In many instances, you are sharing your soul, so it's no wonder you aim for perfection. But perfectionism takes its toll.

On the one hand, you work yourself to the bone and never feel that what you are doing is good enough. You then devote all of your time striving for perfection because you are thinking, "If I don't do it perfectly, I am a failure."

On the flip side, perfectionism often means avoiding your work. Perfectionism explains a lot of procrastination because your inner critic causes you to ask, "What is the point of starting? I never am going to do it perfectly."

Perfectionism is another manifestation of the fixed mindset: You hold on to the belief that you have a fixed amount of talent and intelligence and that if you don't do things perfectly, it means you are not talented or smart. Perfectionism is a major roadblock to creative success because it threatens your self-esteem and your ability to trust yourself.

While I have never cured anyone of perfectionism (including myself), as Jake discovered, there are many ways to manage the voice of the inner critic. Here are a few good strategies.

Change the thought: The voice of perfection is simply a thought. Answer back with a more empowering thought, like your flow affirmation or your growth-mindset thoughts.

Change your attitude: Perfectionism carries with it negative judgments: both self-judgment and the judgment of others. Change your attitude by practicing nonjudgment and get in the flow. Meditate. Relax. Allow yourself time to renew.

Be of service: Take the focus off of yourself and consider how you can be of service to others. Dedicate your creative work to a loved one or to the source of your inspiration.

Reframe: Reframe the need to be perfect and instead aspire to be your best self by tapping into your flow self.

Check the extremes: Perfectionism is filled with extremes, so check the need to be perfect.

Beth,* a creative software designer, never responded to emails on time because she thought that every email had to be perfect. She often spent 45 minutes on an email response, and her inbox grew exponentially. By learning to gauge which emails were important, she learned how to sort through her emails more strategically and let go of the need to write the perfect email every time.

Like Beth, you can avoid the extremes of perfectionism as follows:

- Ask yourself how important it is for this task to be completed perfectly.

- Consider what is at stake. Not everything requires 100 percent effort.

- Reflect on how well perfectionism is working for you and what impact it is having on your life. What might you be missing by insisting on perfection?

- Set a time limit for your tasks. You can even set an alarm and stop when the alarm goes off.

Overcome your fear of making the wrong choice: While the future may be uncertain, there is no such thing as the perfect choice. Yet that uncertainty stops many creatives for fear of making the "wrong" choice—another manifestation of perfectionism. Happily, there are ways to manage your fears of making the wrong choice.

- Take stock of your assets.
- Persevere with the growth mindset.
- Work on smaller goals.
- Let go of the results.

Slow down and celebrate: It's hard to achieve big goals, so take the time to celebrate your accomplishments. Slow down. Pause. Acknowledge your success. Figure out how you got there. It shows that you are able to achieve what you set out to do. And it is an important way to get over the voice of your inner critic.

THIRD CREATIVITY KILLER: COMPARE-AND-DESPAIR

Which of the following statements resonates for you?

"He just came back from a world tour and I am still a student."

"All my peers are getting jobs and I am still unemployed."

"Why do I struggle with my craft when my colleagues can do it effortlessly?"

Welcome to compare-and-despair. It attacks many creative people who compete for grants, tenure, official competitions, auditions, jobs, contracts, and the like. It is understandable that you might find yourself making comparisons. To make matters worse, with so many people trumpeting their successes on social media, you might be feeling left out and falling behind. But these comparisons are illusory, not to mention destructive.

One of my old bosses had a great expression: "There is nothing more misleading than the score at halftime." So maybe you are still in the first quarter, let alone at halftime.

If the voice of comparison is holding you back, here are a few ways to combat it:

- Remember that everyone experiences failure. No one is going to post their rejection letters on Instagram.

- Share with trusted friends.

- Identify what makes you unique.

- Focus on what you really want: your vision and goals, not someone else's.

- Chart your progress and start with small successes.

- Get off of social media.

Overcome The Creativity Killers:
Get Better Goals

If you are one of the many creatives out there whose creativity is threatened by one or more of these creativity killers, you need a different and gentle way to accomplish your goals: instead of focusing on being good at something, focus on getting better.

Suppose perfectionism is holding you back. You set a goal to *get better* at managing perfectionism. Then, select one or more of the strategies to overcome perfectionism and take actions each week toward the goal of getting better at managing perfectionism.

Why does this work?

Psychologist Heidi Grant distinguishes between two types of goals: *be-good goals,* through which you set out to prove that you have the ability to perform the task and that you already know what you are doing, versus *get-better goals*, through which you focus on developing your ability and learning new skills.[3]

According to Grant's research, be-good goals carry with them the need to be perfect from the outset. The danger is that the pressure to "be good" often results in poor performance and mistakes, whereas get-better goals enable you to focus on the experience itself, which takes the pressure off of performing. By giving yourself permission to make mistakes and learn from the experience, you are relieving yourself of anxiety, thereby increasing your motivation to succeed. As a result, the chances of making mistakes are dramatically reduced. And your yardstick is *your* prior performance, not someone else's, so you are not competing with others and setting yourself up for more anxiety and failure.[4]

Commit to getting better at managing and overcoming your creativity killer so that you can continue on the road to creative success.

Last Word: Rejection Is Not Failure

You won't believe what happened to Megan.*

Megan was a talented musician with great people skills, a positive attitude, and a deep commitment to her values. She longed to be the dean of a major conservatory, for which she needed a doctorate. By the time she got to graduate school, she had worked her way through her undergraduate degree, earning top academic and musical honors and performing with an award-winning ensemble. She was poised for success.

But in her master's program, things did not go as planned. She received a string of rejections after her orchestral auditions. Her chamber ensemble broke up. On top of that, she was rejected by all but one of her selected doctorate programs, and that program did not offer her enough funding to attend. She was really worried about her future.

That's when she came to see me.

"I feel like such a failure," she told me. "My dreams of becoming a dean seem unattainable. I don't have a chamber ensemble anymore, and I can't afford to go to the only doctorate program that accepted me. I am stuck and don't know where I am going with my life."

"It feels terrible to get all these rejections," I responded. "But they do not reflect your self-worth because rejection is not the same as failure. What can help is to go deep into your core values and see what these experiences are teaching you. It's going to be a hard thing, but with your work ethic and commitment to learning, I know you can do this."

So, Megan took stock of her situation and realized that she had a lot going for her. Through all her work experience, she had an impressive array of professional experience. Thanks to her passion for teaching, she had private students. Moreover, because of her commitment to helping those in lesser-served communities, she had a lot of experience as a teaching artist. Slowly, she began to see the possibility of a different path to the future. She deferred her acceptance to the doctorate program and took a job with her university.

Megan also began to reflect on how well a performance career aligned with her values of relationships, community, authenticity, and service. She took one more big audition and did not advance. It felt terrible. And again, she felt like a failure. But then she remembered her values and asked herself, "Is this what I am meant to be doing? Am I really sure that I want an orchestra job?" And by asking this question, she was able to reallocate her energy and explore what really mattered to her.

The following year, she worked, took freelance performing gigs, and continued her private teaching. She also discovered that, without academic obligations, she had free time to do some research. She tapped into her passion for helping the underdog and decided to investigate unknown women and minority composers. Thanks to her excellent network of relationships, she enlisted fellow students and colleagues in her pursuit and organized a series of concerts. And Megan discovered that her true path lay in being of service to communities in need. When the time came to let the doctorate program know whether or not she was coming, the answer was clear: She did not want a doctorate after all.

Instead, Megan sought out work in the nonprofit sector. Because of her commitment to excellence, she had a great track record from her school jobs, with top recommendations from her supervisors. And finally, she landed a great job in arts administration.

I recently caught up with Megan, who was thriving in her new job.

"I learned so much from those perceived failures," she told me. "In fact, my only regret is that I did not allow myself to fail more. These days, I love putting my ideas out there because I know that no matter what happens, I will learn from the experience."

All those rejections led Megan to explore a new path, connect the dots, and find a better fit. And who knows where it may lead?

Rejection does not have to be failure. As Megan learned, if you are committed to your values and to learning, you, too, can plow through the fears and keep going.

At what point do you say "enough"?

That is a question each person must answer for himself or herself. If you are receiving a string of rejections, it may very well be that what you are pursuing is not the right match for you. There are many other ways of making your way as a creative, so look for what works for you.

Penny,* the executive director of an opera company, came to arts administration after a career as a singer. In that role, she experienced a lot of "failure" via rejection and eventually got used to it. But after a certain point, she realized that it was sapping her energy to keep auditioning and not winning roles. That's when she made the decision to transition to arts administration. She started out working in a development role for a small company and then was hired to run a larger organization. Now, in her administrative role, nothing feels like failure. Instead, it might be disappointing when she does not achieve a hoped-for result, but she routinely asks for feedback in order to learn from the experience; then she is able to move on to the next project.

Tom,* a young musician with a wide range of interests, was determined to play in an orchestra and gave himself one year after graduating from his master's program to win an orchestra job. After a year, a discouraged Tom still had no wins under his belt. Instead, he decided to pursue a different route: college student affairs. Building on his own undergraduate experience as a resident advisor, he accepted a job in student affairs at a local university. Today, Tom enjoys his work with college students and performs informally on the side, happy to have a secure job and more life balance.

If you are weighed down by any of the creativity killers, explore these strategies to keep you on track to your creative success.

HOW TO ACHIEVE *CREATIVE SUCCESS NOW*

OVERCOME THE THREE TOP CREATIVITY KILLERS

1. Identify your top fear(s) and specify the nature and source of your fear(s).

2. Weigh the evidence that says you are a failure.

3. Learn from your setbacks.

4. Practice success through small victories.

5. Address perfectionism by changing your negative thoughts.

6. Reframe your attitude toward needing perfection in order to succeed.

7. Celebrate your accomplishments.

8. Refrain from comparing yourself to others.

9. Manage your fear of uncertainty.

10. Set a growth goal to overcome your creative block and focus on getting better, not being good.

11. Consider your tolerance for rejection and what you are learning from that experience.

CHAPTER NINE

Time Management For Creatives

Ariel Horowitz, a passionate, charismatic violinist committed to performing at the highest level, had a busy performance schedule, academic obligations, a social justice project, a wide circle of friends, and a big problem: She was approaching burnout. Her health was suffering, and she was exhausted from cramming too much into her already-packed days and nights.

"I can't go on like this anymore," she said to me one day. "I don't use a calendar because I think I can remember everything and things are starting to fall through the cracks. I know that I need to reprioritize, but I have never been any good at sticking to a schedule. And if it's not perfect, I don't know how to do it."

"How do you set priorities?" I asked.

"I just do the next thing that's ahead of me. I am being pulled in a million directions, trying to please everyone else. And I am losing myself in the process," she responded.

I told her that I could teach her a system to help her focus on the most important things in her life. She sighed with relief and asked me to tell her more.

"Learning how to prioritize takes some work." I explained. "Step one is getting very clear on your top life areas that reflect your values.

Then, you will need to commit to those priorities and not worry about what other people want for you. This means shifting the way you think about yourself and your time. This may seem hard at first, but I am sure that you can do it."

"Let's get started," she said. "I can no longer live like this."

Ariel zeroed in on four areas that were vital to her life: her music career, service, personal development, and health and wellness. Relationships were a close runner-up.

"This is really hard!" she exclaimed. "What if something really exciting comes up later on in the semester and I have to turn it down? And what about seeing my friends? I am worried about missing out on all these other things."

"It's hard to prioritize and say no," I responded. "What helps is to think about what you want to accomplish in the long term. Tell me, what is your vision for the future?"

Without hesitating, Ariel said, "A fulfilling performance career, a flourishing service project, a family and friends whom I love, and a healthy me."

"How impressive that you see your future life," I observed. "It sounds beautiful and certainly reflects your values of excellence, service, and relationships."

"Wow," she remarked. "I never thought about how my values relate to the way I use my time. This does feel different."

"Setting priorities is a bit easier to do when you know your future direction, and you are committed to values-based goals," I told her. "Let's consider what you might need to do this semester to work toward the future that you laid out for yourself."

Ariel made a list of the five top priority activities for the rest of the semester:

1. Music career: Accept only high-impact, artistically fulfilling performances; practice daily to ensure that she could maintain a high level of performing; plan her spring touring schedule.

2. Service: Work on the summer festival that she had founded to teach music to children on a Navajo reservation.

3. Health and wellness: Get enough sleep, exercise three to five days a week, shop for food and cook when at home, and eat healthy food when on the road.

4. Personal development: Create a schedule that allows her to focus her energy on her top priorities.

5. Relationships: Study and go to the gym with friends.

It felt great to focus on activities that pointed her in the direction of her vision of success. Ariel bought a big wall calendar and began to plan on a weekly basis. Then came the really hard part: sticking to the list.

It took a while for her to commit fully to her list of priorities. From time to time, she would slip up and cram in her practice sessions or cut back on sleep. She then had to avoid seeing friends, which made her feel cut off from her community. But she soon got the hang of sticking to the list and felt much more energized and productive.

What helped Ariel were two big concepts:

- Identifying the most important areas of her life to set values-based priorities

- Making a schedule that focused on her important and not urgent matters.

In this way, she was able to commit fully to her holistic vision of success.

Set Values-Based Priorities

Creatives live busy lives that encompass areas beyond their careers. To be successful, it is important to allocate time to your most important life areas. Otherwise, resentments will start to creep in and undermine your energy. What helps is to identify your long-term balance goals and then set priorities that build toward those goals. Be sure that your balance goals reflect your top values. In this way, you are aligning your life with your values.

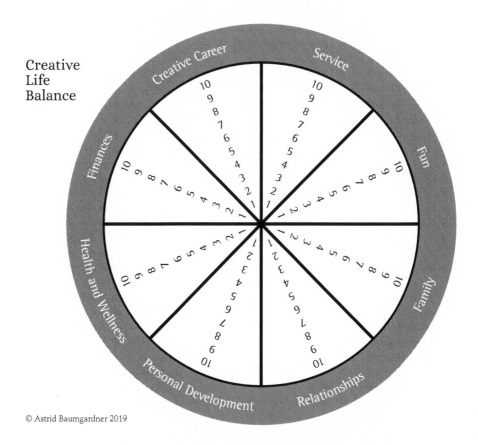

Creative
Life
Balance

© Astrid Baumgardner 2019

And here's the thing: The more your priorities—your short-term goals—align with your inspirational, values-based, long-term goals, the more motivated you will be to achieve them.

To get clear on your priorities, look at the Creative Life Balance Circle[1] and identify the most important elements of your life.

1. Creative Career

2. Service

3. Fun

4. Family

5. Relationships

6. Personal Development

7. Health & Wellness

8. Finances

Feel free to adjust this list to include any other areas that are important to you.

Now, rate each area as follows:

1. How important is each area to you? (1 means "not important," and 10 means "indispensable")

2. How satisfied are you with the amount and/or quality of time you spend in each area? (1 means "not at all satisfied," and 10 means "absolutely satisfied.")

Next, identify areas with gaps of two or more points. This will give you an indication of what you need to work on.

Go back to your three most important areas and consider what you want to accomplish in these big areas. These are your top long-term life balance goals. Be sure that these goals reflect your values.

Notice that Creative Career is one of the eight elements of your life. Go back to your big career goal from chapter 7 and filter it into this wheel to see how that goal stacks up against the other areas that you rated as important.

Creative Quadrant Two Time Management

On to learning the system that will change the way you manage yourself through time: Quadrant Two time management for creatives.

Quadrant Two time management comes from Steven Covey, author of the iconic book, *7 Habits of Highly Effective People.*[2] Covey created a model based on what is important and not important and what is urgent or not urgent, using the following four quadrants:

NOT URGENT

URGENT

Q1 NECESSITY

Crises
Emergency meetings
Last-minute deadlines
Unforeseen events

Q2 EFFECTIVENESS

Proactive work
Important goals
Creative thinking
Planning and prevention
Relationship building
Learning and renewal
Recreation

Q3 DISTRACTION

Needless interupptions
Unnecessary reports
Irrelevant meetings
Other people's minor issues
Unimportant tasks, phone
  calls, status posts, etc.

Q4 WASTE

Trivial work
Avoidance activities
Excessive relaxation,
  television, gaming, internet
Time-wasters
Gossip

IMPORTANT

NOT IMPORTANT

© 2004 Stephen R. Covey, *The 7 Habits of Highly Effective People* (Simon & Schuster 2004)[3]

Under this model, you change the focus to attend to the activities, projects, and areas of your life that are important to you (Quadrant Two), reduce the amount of time you spend dealing with immediate deadlines and crises (Quadrant One), minimize activities that interrupt or divert you from your important work (Quadrant Three), and eliminate pure time-wasters (Quadrant Four).

BONUS: To help you organize your own activities, download the Creative Quadrant Two Worksheet from my website at creativesuccessnow.com/CreativeQuadrantTwoWorksheet.

QUADRANT ONE: URGENT AND IMPORTANT

Quadrant One (Q1) activities are the deadline-driven, crisis-oriented, pressing obligations like papers, presentations, rehearsal, performances, and anything else that has an immediate deadline. We tend to spend most of our time in this quadrant. Quadrant One activities are often reactionary and very stressful: the opposite of choice-based work. Spending too much time in this quadrant is a fast recipe for burnout. To achieve greater balance, aim to reduce the amount of time that you spend on these activities.

QUADRANT TWO: NOT URGENT—IMPORTANT

Quadrant Two (Q2) is where you create your long-term vision: cultivating and nurturing important relationships, planning, devoting time to personal and professional development, setting long-term goals, relaxing, and spending time on creative refreshers.

Accomplishing Q2 activities can be challenging because no one (other than you) cares if you accomplish these tasks. Moreover, there are no external deadlines. Instead, it is up to you to decide what is important and then slot in a few Q2 activities each week on which you can focus. This is how to become proactive, positive, and effective at accomplishing your important goals.

You will feel a lot better about your time if you spend at least 10 percent of your day in Quadrant Two. Ideally, aim to devote 30 percent of your day to Quadrant Two activities.

One helpful way to bring more Q2 into your life is to identify activities on your immediate Q1 to-do list that help you build your Q2 vision. The more closely aligned Q1 and Q2 are, the better you feel about what you are doing, and the less stress you will experience when tackling Quadrant One.

QUADRANT THREE: URGENT—NOT IMPORTANT

Do you sometimes feel that you have been busy all day, but as you look back on your day, you feel that you have not accomplished anything? Chances are that you have spent too much time on Quadrant Three (Q3) activities: things that are important to other people but not important to you.

Quadrant Three includes things like:

- Interruptions like phone calls, "urgent" emails, and text messages
- Meetings that don't matter to you
- Other people's demands on you
- Joining committees or ensembles that you don't really want to be in
- Saying yes to social engagements for fear of saying no

So, minimize these activities. Be aware of what you say yes to. Plan accordingly. Again, by minimizing Q3 activities, you free yourself to spend more time on Q2 activities.

QUADRANT FOUR: NOT URGENT—NOT IMPORTANT.

Jim,* one of my former students, would go home for lunch and start watching his favorite TV series on Netflix. The problem was that he could not stop and often watched seven episodes at a time. Then he had no time to practice or socialize with friends. This is classic Quadrant Four behavior: when you zone out and waste time. It's a pleasure in the moment that does not amount to anything important. Quadrant Four (Q4) often involves activities that we engage in because we are too tired to do anything else, such as:

- Numbing out on the internet
- Spending endless time on social media
- Mindlessly eating junk food
- Binging on movies or television series
- Worrying about the future
- Procrastinating to avoid doing a hard or unpleasant task

While taking a break is important (and, in fact, is a Q2 activity), it's easy to get carried away as Jim did, since engaging in these activities often spills over into hours of wasted time. Jim discovered that once he set a timer and watched two episodes of his favorite show on Netflix, his whole afternoon opened up for practicing and socializing. Watching Netflix became a way to relax (a Q2 activity) as opposed to a time waster (a Q4 activity). If you eliminate Q4, just think of all the time you have for your Quadrant Two activities.

Follow these four steps to implement Quadrant Two time-management into your life.

1. Select and slot in your Quadrant Two activities

2. Manage your Quadrant One activities and see which ones you can reframe as Q2s

3. Reduce Quadrant Three activities

4. Eliminate Quadrant Four activities

By following this model and focusing on Q2, you will be amazed at how much better you will feel about your time as you take those steps toward achieving your important goals.

Implement Your Top Priorities

The next step is to plan your activities so that each week you are working toward your Quadrant Two vision.

First, because priorities are short-term goals, pick a time period for your Q2 list (one month, one semester, one quarter). Then, answer four questions and jot down a specific activity or area of focus:

1. What is the most important thing in my life in this time period? (Q2)

2. Where would I want to spend more time? Less time? (Q2/Q1)

3. What areas need my attention now (e.g., school, talent, health, relationship)? (Q1/Q2)

4. What do I keep putting off doing that I long to do? (Q2)

Now come up with your list of Q2 priorities, consisting of *no more than five* major activities.

It might feel hard to limit yourself to just five major activities. Remember that priorities are short-term goals that will change depending on the time of year (summer, school year, holidays), the projects you are working on at any given time, important circumstances in your personal life, and new opportunities that may arise.

Moreover, your priorities may change over time. A few years ago, I ran a time management workshop with alumni of Ensemble Connect, the prestigious teaching artist fellowship at Carnegie Hall.[4] These young people were ambitious, talented and accomplished musicians who had spent two years in the fellowship when they were just out of graduate school and were now professional musicians in their early-to-mid-thirties. The first person I saw was a very pregnant woman whose due date was that day. And when the participants completed the Creative Life Balance Circle, every single person (male and female) gave the highest rating to family (which in some cases was higher than their rating for their music careers).

Be sure to look at your list of priorities every few months and adjust according to what is the most important thing for you at this time.

JUST SAY NO

Once you have created your priorities and committed to doing them, say no to anything that is not on the list. Remember that this list is not forever; it's your list for now.

Saying no is really hard. We tend to say yes to other people because we want to be seen as reliable and we don't want to disappoint other people. We want people to like us. We don't want to miss out on tempting new opportunities.

The downside is that each time you say yes to someone else, you are falling into Quadrant Three, with less time for your Quadrant Two activities. Moreover, if you do not really care about this activity, you will feel resentful and unmotivated.

Next time, before you say yes, consider how well saying yes matches up with your values, your Q2 priority list, and your important goals. Finally, when you do say no, do so without apologies, because saying no is a considered choice. In effect, you are saying yes to yourself. So give yourself permission to say no.

Concrete Creative Time-Management Strategies

To reinforce your Quadrant Two planning, here are a few additional strategies.

WEEKLY PLANNING

Each week, set aside time to plan. Weekly planning takes the guesswork out of your schedule and will actually save time.

Get out your calendar (if you don't have a calendar, now is the time to get one). First, block out activities to which you are already committed. Then, look for your periods of uncommitted time and slot in one or more Q2 activities.

Some people like to write each task down on the calendar. Other people prefer to log in only major commitments. If there is something that you might overlook, book an appointment with yourself on your calendar.

MAKE A STRATEGIC DAILY TO-DO LIST

Instead of the "kitchen sink" method of dumping everything onto a sheet of paper, create a written, well-prioritized, daily to-do list. Every day, review your upcoming activities as follows:

1. What is the most important thing about today?

2. What must get done today?

3. What is important about the future that I want to do today?[5]

This will help you to accomplish your short-term needs as well as make sure that you are building toward your future.

FOCUS ON THE HIGHEST-IMPACT ACTIVITIES

Another way to pare down your daily list is to look for the highest-impact activities.

Two strategies work like a charm:

Follow the 80/20 rule: The 80/20 rule posits that 80 percent of your results come from 20 percent of your effort. By focusing on what has the biggest impact on your time, you can maximize the use of your time. Look at your to-do list of ten things and identify the two highest-impact activities.

Eat that frog: What is the biggest, yuckiest, most challenging thing on your to-do list? The one most likely to lead to procrastination? Productivity expert Brian Tracy, in his best-selling book, *Eat That Frog*, urges us to swallow the frog and do the most challenging task first. Then the rest of your to-do list will feel like a breeze.[6]

MINIMIZE EXTERNAL DISTRACTIONS

In our wired age of 24/7 availability and connectivity, it is easy to avoid work because it's more "fun" to chat with friends or surf the Internet. You can minimize external distractions with these strategies:

- Block out times to work and turn off your phone, your web browser, and your email.

- Schedule a time each day to respond to email and voice mail and set a timer to stay within your time limit.

- Use the 80/20 rule for email.

- Write down any thoughts that come up while you are working on one project and handle them later.

- Take a break when you are on overload.

Chapter 10

Create Your Personal Brand

Florrie Marshall, a charismatic and enthusiastic musician and teaching artist, had a lot going for her. She had just graduated with a master's degree from Yale, where she had won a prestigious prize, and she was determined to create a unique vision for how to be an artist in today's world.

Florrie was doing a lot, from touring, performing and teaching, to interviewing mentors, and experimenting with a new form of community storytelling. But she was worried. Uncertain about her future, she was struggling to figure out how to continue her connection to the university that she loved. And she felt unmoored with all her activities and worried about how to fit all the pieces of her life together.

That's when Florrie came to me, her former teacher, to discuss her problem.

"I'm running around doing a million things, and I don't know where to put my focus," Florrie told me. "I am stalled on updating my website, I'm not sure which performance engagements to accept, and I can't figure out my next big project. I wish I could figure out how it all ties together."

I reminded her about our class branding exercise: to find the through-line of all her activities and connect her with her ideal audiences. So, we sat down to create her brand statement.

We first looked at what made Florrie unique and memorable to the people with whom she worked. The words that came up were *innovative* and *compassionate*. We examined her activities and identified the common threads in all her activities: curating stories, building upon her musical lineage, and inspiring willing learners. We identified the people with whom she loved working as communities, fellow artists, and willing learners. Finally, we took a look at her purpose and articulated her emotional connection to her audiences: to create an artistic tapestry of human experience fostering a more empathetic world.

She put these elements together to generate the following brand statement:

> *I am an innovative and compassionate artist and teacher who curates stories from communities and fellow artists and builds upon my musical lineage by inspiring willing learners to create an artistic tapestry of human experience fostering a more empathetic world.*

With that, she felt an enormous sense of relief and a renewed motivation to channel her work and connect with her ideal target population. She updated her website.[1] She chose to accept meaningful performance opportunities where she could generate a sense of empathy and compassion. She began working on a new community storytelling project. And she felt motivated and inspired to teach and work with others to create a more compassionate world.

What Is A Brand?

As Florrie learned, creative success depends on your ability to connect with the very people whose lives you want to touch so that they will hire you. That's the essence of a brand.

Branding started in the world of consumer goods to telegraph the best qualities of a product so that consumers will remember it and associate the product with those qualities.

Think Nike: *Just Do It.*

Thanks to Tom Peters, a management guru, we now have the concept of *personal* branding: your promise to the marketplace about what makes you unique and memorable.[2]

A brand is a message that distinguishes you from your competition by expressing what makes you unique and memorable so that your target audience connects with you emotionally and wants to work with you.

WHY CREATIVES NEED A PERSONAL BRAND

Be yourself—everyone else is already taken.
—Oscar Wilde

A brand can help your creative success in a number of ways.

Branding builds confidence. Jenna Siladie, a soprano, was nervous about her upcoming auditions for an agent. Just as she was going out on stage for her first audition, she silently repeated her brand statement to herself. Suddenly, a wave of stillness swept over her. She tapped into what made her unique and called up her inner strengths and talents instead of fixating on weaknesses. As she sang, she felt true to herself and sensed that her audience of agents was excited to discover a fresh and unique approach. And she landed an agent on her very first audition.

As Jenna discovered, having a brand reinforces your self-knowledge and can serve as a guidepost or motivational tool to help you stay true to the best of who you can be. This enables you to project confidence to those around you. It also inspires you to believe in yourself.

Jenna also found that having a brand helps you to see yourself as unique and can overcome the perception that you are just one of thousands of creatives out there. This too reduces the pressures of competition.

Branding helps shape your career. As a creative, having a brand is a profound way to connect with your creative output and your audience and shapes your career, helping you take it to a new level.

For example, many musicians I know are eager to shake up the world of classical music and do something out of the box in their career. How they succeed depends on their knowing what specifically makes them great, and then identifying the audiences who will appreciate their unique offerings.

The members of the young and versatile Argus String Quartet are quickly emerging as important voices on the classical music scene. They won the 2017 M-Prize Chamber Arts Competition and are now under management with Concert Artists Guild. Argus is dedicated to "reinvigorating the audience-performer relationship through innovative concerts and diverse programming." The quartet collaborates with many of today's leading composers while honoring the traditions of the classical music chamber canon in the service of its mission "to connect with and build up a community of engaged listeners, with the strong belief that today's ensembles can honor the storied chamber music traditions of our past while forging a new path forward."[3]

Branding helps you work smarter and not harder. A brand helps you zero in on the people with whom you most want to connect. With that knowledge, your efforts are focused on the specific people you want to attract, as opposed to trying to appeal to the entire world. This means you are working smarter, not harder.

Create Your Brand

Create your personal brand by answering these four questions:

1. How am I unique?

2. How is what I do distinctive?

3. Who is my ideal audience?

4. Why should we work together?

BONUS: To help you create your brand, download the Create Your Personal Brand worksheet from my website at creativesuccessnow.com/CreateYourPersonalBrandWorksheet.

The first two elements of a brand statement focus on *you*.

Step One: How am I unique? A personal brand articulates the specific qualities you possess that make you stand out from the competition. To begin, therefore, you must start by defining what is unique or unusual about you. Come up with words that describe what you are like at your best. Then, think about what other people remember about you and how they would describe the experience of working with you.

A great way to figure out your uniqueness is to find a tangible object that says something special about you and articulate those qualities.

Ashley Smith, who is passionate about opera and new music, selected a concert video of Cecilia Bartoli singing Vivaldi. He saw this video when he was eight years old and it inspired him to go into music. He also said that if he could be anyone else, it would be Cecilia Bartoli because she is "insanely gifted, has amazing technique, and is generous as a performer." Combining his passion for the new with his admiration for Cecilia Bartoli, he described himself in his brand statement as follows:

I am a generous, charismatic, and innovative musician who takes risks and stretches the boundaries of the art form whilst always striving for the highest possible level of technical accomplishment.

Step Two: How is what I do distinctive? The next step is to look at yourself as a whole, beyond your professional arena, and examine what your outside interests say about who you are.

Lots of creatives I know love to cook. So here are two different takes. Richard,* the composer, loves to cook refined meals and try new things. His brand words are *novel, spare,* and *precise.* Mark,* the conductor, likes to cook by using whatever ingredients he has on hand. His brand words are *resourceful, innovative,* and *creative.*

Sports also provide a useful arena for defining your brand qualities. Ann,* the violinist, was a competitive swimmer in high school and describes herself as *competitive, accurate,* and *rhythmic.* Jesse,* the pianist, is a competitive triathlete and describes himself as *fast, razor-sharp,* and *passionate.*

Step Three: Who is my target audience and why am I the best person to satisfy their needs? The third step in creating a personal brand is identifying your target audience. This step clarifies your objectives, so you can map your career path as efficiently as possible.

David Perry, a clarinetist deeply committed to community engagement, felt liberated in targeting his ideal audience rather than trying to appeal to everyone. He defined that audience as his community band students and their families who were looking for community-building through music. David realized that he was passionate about teaching and performing for this audience since they did not care about his competition wins or his pedigree. Instead, they valued his personal qualities. In turn, he cared deeply about them. This insight helped him to feel more confident to shape his career toward community. After he graduated from Yale, David created a concert series in New Haven, performed and worked as a teaching artist, and today teaches at a university, where he continues to engage with his local community.

To identify your target audience, create a profile of one individual who represents the ideal audience member for whom you most want to create your work. Then, consider what your target audience is looking for that *only you* can provide.

This is the secret of creative branding: figuring out the people to whom you feel connected. As David discovered, you feel energized when you reach out and connect to those with whom you feel an affinity. You can be yourself, and the fear of marketing dissipates with the knowledge that you are offering your services to the very people who need you.

Step Four: Why do I do what I do? The last step in creating your personal brand is to commit to your brand on an emotional level in order to connect deeply with your target audience.

CHAPTER 11

Enjoy Networking

Heather,* a musician and teaching artist with a gentle, lovely manner, felt stalled in her freelance music and teaching career. She was frustrated that she was not getting a lot of performance opportunities, so she took on some administrative work at one of the schools where she was teaching. She then began applying for jobs in arts administration but was not getting callbacks for these jobs, either. That's when she sought my help.

"I don't know how to move forward," she confided in me. "My friends and peers seem to be getting good work, and I feel way behind. Nothing I do is good enough. And I don't seem to know the right people."

"It sounds as though you need help building your own network," I answered.

Heather remarked that she didn't think she could learn how to network. She also thought that if she had to ask other people for help, they would think that she was a loser. She confessed that she simply did not have the confidence to go out there and meet new people.

I could see that she needed a lot of help.

"There is a lot that you can do to build your network, but it's going to take some work," I told her. "We first have to boost your confidence, and then you will need to learn some networking skills. What do you think?"

"Well," she said, "The reason I want to work with you is that you help a lot of successful people whom I admire, so I guess it's OK to ask you for help."

I explained that networking is not about asking for help. Instead, networking is a long-term strategy of creating a mutually supportive circle of business friends who share resources and contacts.

The first step for Heather was to start with someone safe and to concentrate on the people she already knew. Her assignment was to set up a meeting with someone who was doing something that sounded interesting, inquire about that person's career, and ask for suggestions he or she might have for her.

Two weeks later, she came back and reported that she had made dates with three people. And that it was not so hard. Over the next few months, she contacted more people, going beyond her immediate circle of friends. And she started to get hired. Her freelance career was moving ahead. I even went to see her in a few of her performances.

Then one day, she told me that she had applied for a very interesting job running the education program of a nationally recognized arts organization. She didn't know anyone there, but she was sure she could do the job.

She was right. Not only did she get an interview, but she landed the job.

The difference?

In her past job applications, she was fearful and displayed a negative attitude. This time, she felt much more confident.

"Now that I have the hang of networking," she shared, "I feel good about the process, and I am putting out much more positive energy. I'm in the right space to go into networking mode. And networking pays off."

What Is Networking?

In-person networking is one of the best ways to advance your creative career. Yet, for many people, networking is a terrifying experience, giving rise to thoughts like:

"Networking feels fake, and I hate selling myself."

"I'm too afraid to introduce myself to strangers."

"Why would some famous person want to talk to me?"

If that sounds like you, it is time to reframe the experience of networking. My favorite definition of networking has nothing to do with fake selling. Instead, networking is "connecting with another person so that the two of you can share and remain relevant to each other."

Think of networking as an opportunity to share yourself as you expand your community and remain relevant to people with whom you felt a personal connection. And then consider that networking is a skill that you can acquire and master with practice.

WHY NETWORKING IS IMPORTANT FOR CREATIVES

Grammy-nominated composer Adam Schoenberg, twice named among the top ten most-performed living classical composers by orchestras in the United States, enjoys a thriving career.[1] While he was finishing up his doctorate at Juilliard and living in Miami, Adam figured out a way to meet Maestro Robert Spano (music director of the Atlanta Symphony Orchestra) when he was working in Miami with the New World Symphony. Adam had researched the Maestro's schedule, so he had a good idea of when he might be free to talk. He also knew that Maestro Spano was a smoker, so Adam waited outside of the rehearsal space to introduce himself during a break. Sure enough, Maestro Spano stepped outside for a cigarette, and Adam introduced himself as follows:

"Maestro, we have two things in common. We both went to Oberlin." This did not elicit much of a reaction. "Second, I studied orchestration at Juilliard with Chris Theofanidis." This was one of Maestro Spano's former students, who is a well-known composer.

The mention of Chris' name drew an immediate reaction. Spano's eyes lit up, and he invited Adam into the conductor's suite to listen to a piano reduction of Theofanidis's most recent symphony, which Spano played on the fly. The rehearsal break was now over, and the Maestro had to go back into the hall to finish rehearsing, but he invited Adam to lunch the next day. Adam brought the score of one of his compositions, *Finding Rothko,* and gave it to Maestro Spano, who told him to keep in touch by email.

Adam called and emailed, but the Maestro did not respond. But a few months later, Adam got a call from Spano who said that he had loved the piece and would be programming it on the Atlanta Symphony's upcoming season. He also commissioned Adam to write a new work for the symphony. With that, Adam's career took off. He is now a highly successful composer and university teacher.

In the age of the internet and social media, in-person networking remains an important way to advance your career. Not only does networking expand your circle of friends and acquaintances, but it also helps you learn firsthand about opportunities, job openings, performances, and grants. You never know what might happen when you stretch yourself and meet new people.

OVERCOME THE COMMON OBJECTIONS TO NETWORKING

It is important to get the common objections to networking out of the way.

"Networking feels fake." Networking is about creating quality connections. The best way to do that is to be yourself.

"I hate selling myself." Networking is not a sales pitch. Instead, it is a long-term strategy of creating a mutually supportive group of professional friends.

"I hate small talk." Networking is about sharing ideas and information. You don't need to chit-chat. You are there to share and be of service.

In the age of the internet and social media, in-person networking remains an important way to advance your career.

"I'm an introvert and don't have good people skills." If you identify as an introvert, you may think that you do not have the capacity to network because you don't have good people skills. Wrong!

First of all, being an introvert means that you need to replenish yourself after being around a lot of people. Many introverts enjoy quality relationships. To overcome the bias against introverts, Susan Cain, author of the bestseller *Quiet: The Power of Introverts in a World That Can't Stop Talking*, has ushered in the "Quiet Revolution" to help introverts assert their power in our culture.[2] If this sounds like you, be sure to follow Susan and check out her fabulous website.[3]

If you are an introvert, you can network on your own terms. Instead of attending large networking events amid throngs of people, look for opportunities to meet people in small-group situations. Make dates to speak one-on-one in coffee shops or other informal settings. At receptions, talk to one person at a time.

"Why would some famous person bother to talk to me?" That famous person was once a young professional, and someone probably talked to her. People in general love to talk about what they do. Famous people enjoy sharing insights. It's flattering. Plus, you are not asking them for a job. Yes, *some* famous people won't be bothered to talk to a younger colleague; don't take it personally.

"I don't know how to network, and I don't know what to say." Networking is a skill that you can learn by mastering the principles in this chapter. And you are about to learn a technique to help you introduce yourself to others in networking situations.

The Four Principles Of Effective And Effortless Networking

Using our definition of networking, here are the four principles of effective and effortless networking:

1. Prepare

2. Connect

3. Share

4. Remain relevant

PRINCIPLE NUMBER 1: PREPARE

Networking is a combination of using your head to be strategic and using your heart to make a genuine connection. Before you set out to expand your professional circle, it helps to prepare.

Plan your strategy. Decide with whom you want to network. Identify the categories of people whom you would like to meet. Go beyond your immediate professional circles and network with people outside your industry who might have valuable knowledge and skills. Identify your target audience and who might introduce you to your ideal audience members. Figure out where to find the people with whom you want to connect. Think about the types of information and resources that are important to you.

Develop a database of contacts. Next, make a list of everyone you already know. Then, think about contacts who can introduce you to someone with whom you are eager to connect. Networking is a process of degrees of separation. Start with family and friends. Then branch out to include anyone with whom you have studied, worked, or collaborated. Find a few connectors who themselves have large networks and the potential to widen your own circle.

Think broadly about your friends. Don't be shy about reaching out to people with whom you have lost touch. The internet and social media are great ways to reconnect.

Organize your contacts into a database or an excel spreadsheet, including first and last name, email address, phone number, street address and a note on how you met this person. Every time you meet someone new, add him or her into your list.

Create an elevator pitch. For many creatives, a major stumbling block to networking is knowing what to say about themselves when they meet someone new. That is where an elevator pitch can come in handy.

An elevator pitch is a short introduction that tells your listener who you are and what you do in such a way that you stand out from the crowd, so the person with whom you are speaking will want to find out more about what you do, have another encounter with you, and become a part of your network.

An elevator pitch is not intended to get you a job or a gig. As such, it can take the pressure off, since you are not selling yourself. Because networking is about creating quality connections, save your elevator pitch for people with whom you feel a genuine connection.

If you have identified different categories of people whom you want to meet, you will need a number of different elevator pitches. Performers have lots of choices, from presenters, arts administrators, and orchestra managers to other artists and musicians. If you teach, you might want to meet potential students or deans or professors who are in a position to hire you. If you are looking to create an ensemble, you may want to meet potential collaborators and supporters. Since your elevator pitch is focused on your listener, consider what aspects of your life or career would interest that particular person.

Here are the elements of a good elevator pitch:

1. Name, credentials, and how you stand out

2. Your connection to the person with whom you are speaking

3. Your mission/project/goal that will be of interest to your listener

4. What you would like from this encounter

Here is a template for an elevator pitch to help you get started:

My Elevator Pitch

My name is_____and I am _____.
(*Your credentials and what you do*)

I am interested in speaking with you _____.
(*Your connection with this person*)

I am currently working on/my passion/my goal _____
(*Your project or goal or mission that may be of interest to this person*)

May I _____ ¿
(*Your goal from this encounter*)

For more details on how to create an elevator pitch, consult *Creative Success Now: The Workbook*.

Frame a safe goal. Create a goal and a plan for achieving your networking goal. A safe goal is to meet one or two new people or learn a specific piece of information.

Be proactive. Don't sit back and wait for people to contact you. Be on the lookout for the right opportunities to meet the people and acquire the information that you need to succeed.

Think expansively about where to network. Networking can happen anywhere. In addition to the obvious places like professional receptions, festivals, and competitions, you can network anytime you meet people whose lives interest you. My students and colleagues have successfully networked on train and plane rides, at social gatherings unrelated to music, in carpools on the way to gigs, and with audience members.

PRINCIPLE NUMBER 2: CONNECT

Be yourself. Jill Grafflin, a dynamic creative marketing executive at American Express, felt stuck in a middle-management position and did not know how to get ahead. She consulted me to help her transition to a new career. As she learned more about how to adopt a positive mindset and tap into her values and strengths, she became more comfortable asserting her ideas at work. She proactively went after projects that played to her strengths. With her newfound confidence, she began networking with people in her organization beyond her immediate team. Her bosses noticed how valuable she was and she soon was promoted. Today, Jill enjoys a flourishing career heading up the European branch of her company's business. As she told me, "Once I was comfortable being myself, a whole world of opportunity opened up for me."

As Jill learned, the best way to connect with others is when you present yourself authentically.

Tap into your authenticity set from chapters 5 and 6. Remind yourself of your passions. Play to your strengths. Align with your values and your purpose.

Networking is an opportunity to show people the best side of you. And since networking is about making quality connections, this is an invitation for you to be authentic as well. People can sense if you are not genuine, so don't pretend to be something that you are not.

Have a positive attitude. Successful networking requires a positive attitude and confidence. It helps to play to your strengths while networking. If you are blessed with good people skills, networking can be a lot of fun. If you like to think and strategize, networking is an opportunity to use those skills as well. If you love to learn, networking creates myriad opportunities for acquiring new information and learning from others. Remember to tap into your flow self and to share your passions, since passion is infectious.

How to connect. Start with someone safe. Look for a friend or someone you already know who is speaking to someone you do not know. When you are meeting new people, instead of barging in and talking about yourself, listen first. Focus on the other person and pay attention to what he or she is saying. Find areas of common interest, ask questions, and show genuine interest in that person.

Focus on quality, not quantity. Some people think that networking means showing up at an event, meeting a lot of people, and handing out your business card at large. While glad-handing may work for some people, it is not the best way to make genuine connections. Instead, focus on meeting a few people whom you genuinely like and with whom you want to stay in touch.

PRINCIPLE NUMBER 3: SHARE

Networking is about sharing, not about getting. Too many people approach networking situations with the goal of getting hired for something or selling themselves. This attitude translates into pushiness and arrogance. If you think about networking as an opportunity to share, it takes a lot of the pressure off.

Successful networking is a two-way street. When you meet new people, think of how you can be of service. You can share information, contacts, and resources that could be interesting, relevant, or useful to the person with whom you are speaking. If you feel that you have made a nice connection and you see an opening, use your elevator pitch to tell the person something about yourself.

PRINCIPLE NUMBER 4: REMAIN RELEVANT

Once you have made contact with someone whom you would like to make part of your network, keep in touch. Have a business card handy with your name, title, and contact information. Be sure to follow-up with everyone with whom you have connected. If the person has shared resources or information, thank the person and let him or her know how things turned out, especially when the information was particularly helpful. If the person has invited you to meet or asked you to send a CD or another sample of your creative work, do it right away. Keep the person informed about what you are doing. Send out written thank-you notes to everyone who helps you. Start a newsletter and update your new friends about your activities. Send a holiday greeting to everyone in your community. Invite people to your concerts or other events. Networking is a lifelong pursuit, so be sure and cultivate those relationships.

What if your efforts fall flat? If you are not connecting, shake hands and move on to someone else. You are not going to connect with every person you meet. In fact, some people are simply not receptive to networking. Remember that for such people, it is not about you, so you need not take it personally if they do not want to speak to you.

On the other hand, if you were unable to make *any* connections, figure out what part of your approach did not work and try something new the next time. Networking takes practice. The more you do it, the better you will get.

Be patient. It takes time to create an effective network. You are investing in long-term results. As a creative, you know how to practice and prepare and work hard. Networking is another skill that takes time as you create an effective strategy and break it down into manageable bits.

Informational Interviews

The informational interview is an informal conversation with someone working in an area of interest to you. It's an excellent career-building strategy for creative people since you can find out from an insider what it takes to build your career path, discover new and different career options, and learn about the realities of working in your chosen profession. In addition to being a source of firsthand information that is not otherwise available, it is also a way to expand your network with someone whose career you admire.

The goal is not a job interview, but to obtain information and make a genuine connection. You may feel awkward making arrangements to talk with people you don't know about their work. But most people actually enjoy taking a few moments out of their day to reflect on their professional life and giving advice to someone with an interest in their field.

Prior to conducting the interview, research your candidate and prepare some questions to be used as a guide. At the interview, be flexible and open-minded in order to follow new areas that may arise in the course of your interview. Respect the person's time. Solicit her advice and see if she is willing to introduce you to other people in the field. After the interview, thank the person, write a thank-you note, and keep the person informed of your activities so that you can cultivate your relationship with your interviewee.

To learn more about setting up, preparing for, conducting and debriefing an informational interview, be sure to consult *Creative Success Now: The Workbook*.

HOW TO ACHIEVE *CREATIVE SUCCESS NOW*

NETWORKING FOR CREATIVES

1. Examine your attitude toward networking and how it has impacted your career.

2. Decide whom you would like to include in your professional circle and plan your networking strategy.

3. Develop your database of contacts.

4. Create your elevator pitches.

5. Consider what opportunities you have to meet new people and proactively begin to network.

6. Tap into your strengths and passions the next time you meet someone new.

7. Use your flow affirmation to adopt a positive attitude in networking situations.

8. Practice using your elevator pitch when you meet someone with whom you sense a connection.

9. Consider what information, contacts, and resources you can share with people in your network.

10. Follow up with your new contacts and keep them informed of your activities.

11. Be patient as you develop your network and focus on the long-term benefits of having a mutually supportive circle of professional contacts.

12. Conduct an informational interview with someone whose career you admire.

CHAPTER 12

Sustaining Your Creative Life

Nicole,* an active freelance musician and composer, lived in a constant state of fear of not having enough money to live on. She was supporting herself as a full-time performer, and her composition career was also beginning to take off. Yet, she was often strapped for cash. That's when she consulted me.

"I don't understand it," she told me. "I'm busy performing all around New York, I am touring, I have plenty of recording session work, and I am already making some money composing for film and ad agencies. Yet I'm struggling to meet my expenses."

I asked Nicole if she had ever tracked her spending. She responded that she didn't have the time. But here is what really was stopping her: She was terrified at what she might find.

I told her that many people were afraid of what might turn up after tracking their spending. But it was also the first step to cleaning up one's finances and learning how to create a sustainable financial plan. And Nicole was ready to dig in.

The first step was to download a good financial app like Mint and enter her expenses.[1] After a few days, she would start to see patterns. For the next two weeks, Nicole tracked her expenses by category. It was not as hard or as time-consuming as she had feared. And that's when she discovered her black hole: spending money on food and drinks with her fellow performers after every rehearsal and performance.

At our next session, Nicole shared that she had been completely unaware of how much these meals and drinks added up. In addition, by going out every night, she was not getting enough sleep, and her lifestyle was starting to cut into her productivity. That's when she told me about another fear: that if she said no, she would never get asked back for the next round of performances and she might miss out on a big opportunity. I asked her how true it was that her social and performance life would dry up if she said no. She responded, "Most of these outings are a waste of time."

After that, she limited her post-performance outings to times when she would be more likely to expand her network. As for the feeling that saying no would end her social life, she learned that she could say no without apology by explaining to her friends that she needed to get up early the next day and that she would be happy to join them the next time.

The result? Not only did her bank account grow, but she expanded her network, and her performance career has blossomed. And she felt a greater sense of freedom.

The Three Steps Of Financial Freedom

Financial freedom is a function of three elements: A healthy attitude toward your finances, knowledge of basic financial concepts (known as financial literacy), and financial planning.

STEP ONE: EXAMINE YOUR ATTITUDE TOWARD YOUR FINANCES

The start of your financial freedom is to examine your attitudes toward your finances and discover what is holding you back.

What's the first thing that you think of when you think about your finances?

"Dread."

"I don't want to think about it."

"I don't know where to begin."

Money is an emotional topic that often stems from how you were raised to think about money. Your attitude about money says a lot about how you make, spend, and save your money.

In my experience, the four biggest areas that hold creatives back from taking the reins over their finances are fear, uncontrolled spending, debt, and lack of knowledge about how to manage finances.

You can discover your attitude toward your finances by taking the Financial Freedom Quiz in *Creative Success Now: The Workbook*.

To be successful, it is important to face your challenges. And by facing these fears, you are on your way to doing something about your financial situation. So, on to the next step: financial literacy.

STEP TWO: BECOME FINANCIALLY LITERATE

When Clara Kim, an entrepreneurial violinist and member of the Argus String Quartet, was at Yale, she was terrified of running out of money.[2]

As she explained to me, "I'm no good at managing money. I have never done a budget. I don't know how to save or invest. I just don't know what to do."

The good news for Clara was that every year at Yale, we run a financial workshop for graduating students on the basics of financial literacy and planning. Clara attended the workshop and learned about budgeting, saving, and investing. "That wasn't so hard," she told me afterward. "I now know what to do." She began saving and opened an IRA with a local investment manager. And she feels a lot more secure about her future.

One of the top fears is not knowing how to manage your money. The good news is that not knowing how to manage your finances is a skill gap that can be closed through education, not a moral failing that you are doomed to live with forever. You can achieve basic financial health by mastering the following skills.

To become a financially literate creative, master these five topics:

1. Budgeting
2. Spending
3. Savings and debt
4. Investing
5. Taxes

Budget wisely. A budget is a tool that lays out your expenses and your income for a fixed period of time (a month, a quarter, or a year) based on past experience and best estimates. Your goal is to earn more than you spend and to live within your means by carefully tracking your income and expenses on a regular basis. A budget is not a long-term exercise; it is instead a tool to help you manage your financial position in the immediate future. And a budget is based on a lot of assumptions of which you need to be aware at all times, including how you will generate your revenues and what your lifestyle requires.

Spend wisely. One of the benefits of doing a budget is seeing how much you spend versus how much you earn. A helpful mantra is, "Spend only what you do not save." If you are devoted to your creative work, you may have to live leanly, so avoid the temptation of "emotional" spending. If you had a bad day and then "reward" yourself with the latest tech gadget, that won't get you a job. And just think how many gigs you need to have in order to earn all that money. Moreover, avoid credit card debt, which can put you in the hole. Learn the difference between needs and wants. When you don't make a lot of money, you need to be very clear about your spending habits and priorities if you want to be able to live out your dream of being a creative and having a financially secure life.

Save wisely. Since so many creatives are self-employed and have income that fluctuates, it is imperative to start saving now. Many creatives live leanly and wonder how they can save. But small expenses add up. Consider the latte factor: $2 per day for a latte=$800 per year.[3] That money can instead go toward your savings. If you start saving small amounts now, those savings can accumulate very nicely over your lifetime thanks to compounded interest. Even though interest rates might be low right now, it still makes sense to start saving now. For practical tips on how to start saving, consult 360 Degrees of Financial Literacy, a website of the American Institute of Certified Public Accountants (CPAs).[4]

At a minimum, begin to put money away for a rainy-day fund consisting of six months of living expenses. Then, start saving for your retirement using vehicles like the IRA or the Roth IRA.

Invest wisely. If you save money and put it under your mattress, it is not going to get you very far. So, learn the basics of investing. A great way to get started is to consult the online resource, *How Millennials Can Get Rich Slowly*.[5]

Investing is a long-term strategy. Historically, investing money in equities over the long term leads to growth in your portfolio. This involves taking some risk with your money. You can also get investment advice from online brokerage companies and/or through different investment vehicles, exchange-traded funds (ETFs), and mutual funds. Financial institutions like Fidelity, Vanguard, and Schwab have websites with many resources on how to invest.[6]

Pay taxes wisely. Everyone has to pay taxes on earnings if your annual earnings are above a certain threshold. If you have a salaried, full-time job, your employer will deduct your taxes from your paycheck. If you are self-employed, you are responsible for paying your taxes. If you are self-employed, it pays to hire an accountant who can advise you on what expenses to deduct, as well as other tax-saving strategies. One of my former students, Alex,* was able to get into New York City public housing thanks to advice from his accountant.

STEP THREE: MAKE A FINANCIAL PLAN

Now that you know the basics of financial literacy, your final step toward financial freedom is to make a financial plan.

BONUS: Download the Financial Freedom Plan from my website at creativesuccessnow.com/FinancialFreedomPlan.

Set financial goals based on best assumptions. Good financial planning starts by examining your career goals and figuring out how to generate the income to make those goals happen.

You should also consider your lifestyle and your financial objectives. Be sure you are clear on what assumptions you are making regarding your direction forward.

Calculate your annual expenses. With your career goals in front of you and your assumptions at hand, calculate your annual expenses based on your best estimate of living and career-related expenses.

Select your revenue streams. Now, select the revenue streams you are most likely to generate to support yourself as a creative. For many creatives, you will most likely be earning money from multiple sources, and you will not have a full-time job with benefits.

To generate income, consider these two principles:

- **Think expansively about your sources of income.** In addition to traditional sources of creative revenues, go beyond the marquis jobs of tenure-track teaching, performing on Broadway, or singing at the Metropolitan Opera. You can also derive income from full-time or part-time jobs, freelancing fees, grants, royalties, brand-related revenue, merchandising, teaching, workshops, and many more.[7]

- **Plan on multiple revenue streams.** Many creatives rely on more than one source of employment and juggle multiple roles. Therefore, creatives need to plant a lot of seeds in many different fields and diversify their sources of work and revenues. In the words of Josh Quillen, a member of the successful percussion quartet Sō Percussion, you must be "too small to fail." Be sure to have a range of income sources in case one source dries up.

Research the salary ranges of your revenue-generating activities. Next, figure out how much money you can make from each of your revenue streams. If you are already deriving income from performing or teaching, you know how much you can earn per gig or how much you can charge for an hour-long lesson. You can also research salary ranges from the internet or by asking mentors, trusted friends, and colleagues.

Calculate your annual income. To calculate your annual income, take each revenue stream. Identify the charge per service, the number of services per month, and the number of months per year to derive your annual income from this revenue stream. And be sure to be realistic about how much work you can juggle at any one time, how often you can perform, or how many students you can handle.

Let's say that you currently are a substitute player for your local orchestra and each time you rehearse or play, you earn $100. On average, you sub twice a month, and you perform seven months per year. Next year, you will be pursuing your DMA, and you assume that you will have more time to perform so that you will give four performances a month and perform ten months a year. Your income from orchestra performances is calculated as follows:

$$\$100 \text{ (charge per service)} \times 4 \text{ (services per month)} \times$$
$$10 \text{ (months per year)} = \$4,000$$

Do this for each of your revenue streams.

If the total of all of your revenue streams falls short of your annual expenses, think about other ways to derive income. Can you add more students? Charge more per hour? Find new performance opportunities? Now you are thinking like an entrepreneur.

Take action. Think about how you might find sources of work, including networking, introductions from your teachers and mentors, circulating samples of your work, or targeting pitches to organizations whose work dovetails with your own. Implement these strategies by setting a SMART goal and following through with an action step each week.

Review and update your plan. The final step is to review your financial plan on a regular basis to chart your progress. If you have not met your monthly income targets, consider what else you can do to make up the shortfall. You should also assess how well your original assumptions are playing out and make any corrections as you chart your course going forward.

Create Your Support Team

Christine Carter, a brilliant and innovative musician, was at a cross-roads in her doctorate program. With interests in both performance and performance psychology research, she was not sure how to bridge these two pursuits in a typical academic career. She wanted to make sure that a performance career was an important piece in her portfolio of options without sacrificing the academic research she was doing. She was determined to find a way to fit these diverse pieces together and consulted me regarding what she could do to gain clarity on her next steps.

"I am not sure what my options are or where I should focus my efforts," she told me. "My academic research is interesting, but it is outside the normal scope of an applied music university appointment. And I feel that there is more I want to explore in my performance life."

"It sounds as though you could use some outside perspective on what to do next," I observed. "Have you considered forming a personal board of directors?" I asked her.

"What's that?"

"A personal board of directors is comprised of the people in your life who support your vision and to whom you turn when you want honest and trustworthy advice. They can also help you figure out solutions to your challenges. What helps is to have people with a variety of backgrounds and skill sets beyond the world of music," I explained.

The idea was so intriguing that she immediately got to work, reaching out to her chamber music coach (an internationally famous professional musician), a retired business executive, a retired media executive, her childhood best friend, her life partner who was also a musician, and myself, her career coach.

She then went one step further and called a meeting of her personal board to discuss her career challenges. At the meeting, the professional musician quickly responded with the answer about how to embark on a chamber music career. Our meeting might have ended right then and there until the retired business executive offered, "In my world, young people get their careers started by going to Asia." Suddenly, the ideas started flying. We all piped up with observations from our various worlds. When our friend expressed some doubt regarding her ability to pursue some of the strategies, her childhood friend reminded her of various times over the course of their friendship when she had overcome the challenges at hand. Her partner provided an additional layer of reinforcement from her more recent experiences. I was able to coach her into figuring out which of the many ideas would have the biggest immediate impact on her life and what she was prepared to commit to doing.

The end result was a much bigger conversation than Christine had envisioned. She realized that a successful career could involve teaching, developing her expertise in performance psychology through workshops, and continued performance. Most importantly, she felt incredibly supported in her life venture. Ultimately, she spent the rest of her graduate school career solidifying her doctorate research, creating a series of performance psychology workshops, and implementing several creative performance projects. And upon graduation, she won a tenure-track university teaching job and continues to teach, perform, and write and research performance psychology for musicians.[8]

Three Types Of Support Teams

 As you work on your creative success, it helps to have a support team in place. Indeed, the growth mindset teaches that asking for help is a smart strategy.

Here are three top strategies to garner support for your creative endeavors. First, like Christine, you can form a personal board of directors. Next, you can start a mastermind group. Finally, you can hire a career coach.

Support tool number one: Form your personal board of directors. The personal board of directors comes from the business and nonprofit world, where an organization is legally required to have a board of directors to provide guidance and strategic input for optimal functioning of the organization. This concept has been extended to and embraced by individuals who are looking for support and advice from experienced professionals. As Christine learned, having a personal board enables you to learn from professionals whose skills and experience complement your own. It also provides different perspectives to broaden your thinking and provide different points of view, resulting in better decisions. And if you wonder why older, successful, experienced people care about helping someone at the beginning stages of her career, it is incredibly gratifying to give back.

Support tool number two: Start a mastermind group. Another great way to support your creative endeavors is to form a mastermind group—a group of similarly situated peers who meet regularly to discuss the issues around which they want support. The idea came from Napoleon Hill's book, *Think and Grow Rich,* in which he advises budding entrepreneurs to form a group to coordinate their knowledge and efforts as they work together to create success.[9]

Support tool number three: Hire a coach. Hiring a coach is another strategy to help support creative success. A coach is a trusted partner who believes in your success and is there to support your progress. In my own practice, I have helped hundreds of creative people achieve their goals through coaching, both in individual sessions and through group coaching. Consider hiring a coach to work with you individually. Or, like Reena from chapter seven, join a coaching group with like-minded creatives to work toward a common goal under the guidance of a trained coach and receive the support of trusted peers.

HOW TO ACHIEVE *CREATIVE SUCCESS NOW*

SUSTAIN YOUR CREATIVE LIFE

1. Examine your attitude toward your finances and discover what is holding you back.

2. Become financially literate.

3. Create a budget and spending plan.

4. Consider how you can generate revenues as a creative.

5. Start saving and investing.

6. Make your financial plan and begin tracking it against your assumptions and calculations.

7. Form a personal board of directors and reach out to your board members for advice and support.

8. Create a mastermind group with similarly situated creative professionals.

9. Hire a coach for individual coaching.

10. Start a coaching group with like-minded creative professionals and hire a coach to facilitate the sessions.

Summary

To help you cement your learning of the *Creative Success Now* Methodology, here is a brief summary.

In the prologue, we debunked the four top creative myths. You learned that many opportunities exist for creatives to achieve success in today's world and that creativity correlates with indicators of happiness and well-being (chapter 1). You also learned how the *Creative Success Now* Methodology is grounded in principles of positive psychology, and you were introduced to the methodology itself (chapter 2).

In part I, you learned the mindset behind the *Creative Success Now* Methodology. The first element of the mindset is to persevere with a growth mindset (chapter 3). Then, embrace positivity through flow, and be proactive by creating your own opportunities (chapter 4).

In part II, you learned the importance of finding and staying true to your authentic self: you tap into passions, discover and play to your strengths (chapter 5), align with your values, and articulate your purpose (chapter 6).

In part III, you learned about the skill sets that lead to *Creative Success Now*: how to set and achieve inspiring goals (chapter 7), overcome three major creativity killers that can derail you from pursuing your goals (chapter 8), manage yourself through time by focusing on what is most important to you (chapter 9), create your personal brand to distinguish yourself from all the other creatives out there (chapter 10), enjoy networking and create a mutually supportive circle of professional friends (chapter 11), and sustain your creative life by managing your finances and creating your support team of a personal board of directors, a mastermind group, and a coach (chapter 12).

Enjoy your creative journey.

APPENDIX A

Acknowledgments

Writing this book has been an incredible journey of discovery and growth. The idea for this book has been incubating for several years as an outgrowth of my blog, https://www.astridbaumgardner.com/category/blog-and-resources/blog/, which itself reflects my experience teaching and coaching hundreds of creatives to success.

Thank you to my many past and current coaching clients and students at the Yale School of Music, the Juilliard School, the Norfolk Chamber Music Festival, Opera America Leadership Intensive, Carnegie Hall's Ensemble Connect, the Sō Percussion Summer Institute, Pace University's Encore Transition and New Directions Programs, and many others. I appreciate your honest sharing about the highs and the lows of the creative life. It has been an honor to witness your progress and development, and I am so grateful to you for your insights and for your enthusiastic reception of my methodology.

Thank you, Robert Blocker and Paul Hawkshaw, for opening the door to the Yale School of Music and making it possible for me to live out my life purpose by teaching and coaching our amazing students.

Thank you, Megan Walls, for being my mastermind partner and for helping me to be a better coach.

Thank you, Dr. Carol Dweck, for inspiring the foundational principles of this book. I so appreciate your support and encouragement of my work.

Thank you, Amy Wrzesniewski, for your amazing work on job crafting, for sharing your resources, and for encouraging me to write my book.

Thank you, Jennifer Rosenfeld, for coaching me last year on how to write a book and for providing me with so many wonderful resources. You were instrumental in getting the idea out of my head and onto a piece of paper.

Thank you, Alan Cohen, for introducing me to Henry DeVries. Your own example of publishing two books encouraged me to take that big step.

Thank you, Henry DeVries, for your tireless support of my work as my editor and publisher. When I handed you that bulky manuscript last September, I had no idea how to write a good book, and you showed me how to do it. I am so grateful for your wisdom, patience, and good humor for making this an incredible learning experience and a lot of fun. And thanks to the team at Indie Books International for your terrific work in the writing, design, and production stages of my book.

Thank you to the many creatives who contributed their stories to this book. I am so grateful to David Lang, Igor Lichtmann, Barbara Lynne Jamison, Amy Gewirtz, Ashley Smith, Kurt Howard, Anna Friedberg, Jason Treuting, Adam Sliwinski, Josh Quillen, Eric Cha-Beech, Reena Esmail, Dr. Clayton Shiu, Andrea Kornbluth, Tyler Mashek, Russell Fisher, Missy Mazzoli, Ariel Horowitz, Florrie Marshall, Jenna Siladie, David Perry, Adam Schoenberg, Jill Grafflin, Clara Kim, and Christine Carter for sharing your stories and inspiring other creatives to pursue their creative dreams.

Thank you to my many friends who listened to me while I shared my ideas. I am so grateful to Ann Berman for her unfailing ability to pinpoint my challenges and to work with me until we came up with a solution. Thank you, Annette McEvoy, for helping me with design ideas. Thank you, Terry Berenson, for accompanying me on my own creative journey and for always being there for me. Thank you, Ed Yim, for your amazing comments as my reader.

And of course, thank you to my family. Julie Baumgardner and Peter Fusco, you were wonderful sounding boards and always provide invaluable insights on how my ideas resonated with today's millennial creatives. Julie, thanks for your thoughtful insights and comments as another one of my readers. Jeff, thank you for helping me solidify my thoughts on creative leadership. And to my loving husband, John: I could not have completed this project without you. You have always been there to support me throughout my creative evolution and to believe in me even when I had doubts about myself.

Appendix B

About The Author

Astrid Baumgardner, JD, PCC, loves helping creatives to be successful. She brings her experience as a career and executive coach, lawyer, nonprofit executive and consultant, and music board chair to inspire and empower musicians, arts leaders, lawyers, and creative professionals to achieve creative success. A leading voice in arts entrepreneurship, she is on the faculty of the Yale School of Music, where she teaches career entrepreneurship and heads the Office of Career Strategies. As president of her coaching company, Astrid Baumgardner Coaching+Training, she coaches and guest lectures on creative success. She has taught music entrepreneurship at Mannes College of Music at the New School and guest lectures at conservatories and summer music festivals, including The Juilliard School, Norfolk Chamber Music Festival, and the Sō Percussion Summer Institute. She also conducts leadership training workshops at OPERA America and Ensemble Connect, the teaching artist academy at Carnegie Hall.

Ms. Baumgardner's clients and students find that after working with her, they enjoy greater direction, fulfillment, and security. As a result of their work together, her clients and students are thriving as professional musicians, arts leaders, academics, and entrepreneurs.

Ms. Baumgardner enjoys speaking on topics that include Creative Success Now: How to Thrive in the Twenty-first Century; Inspired

Leadership: Flow, Passion and Purpose; Transitioning to a Creative Career; Public Speaking for Musicians; Creativity and Crafting a Life in the Arts; and Creating Successful Music Careers in the Twenty-First Century: Challenges and Opportunities.

She also writes a popular blog on arts entrepreneurship at https://www.astridbaumgardner.com/category/blog-and-resources/blog/.

A graduate of Mount Holyoke College and Rutgers Newark School of Law, where she was a member of the *Law Review*, Ms. Baumgardner practiced law in New York City for twenty-five years. She then combined her professional skills with her love of the arts and served as the deputy executive director of the French Institute Alliance Française of New York. She subsequently became an independent consultant to nonprofit arts boards before starting her coaching business and assuming her position at Yale.

A lifelong amateur pianist and champion of new music, she is a board member and past board chair of Sō Percussion and a board member, past chair, and co-chair of the board of the American Composers Orchestra.

Ms. Baumgardner lives in New York with her husband, John Baumgardner. They have two grown children.

To discuss speaking opportunities or to purchase multiple copies of *Creative Success Now*, please email the author at astrid@creativesuccessnow.com.

Appendix C

The *Creative Success Now* Methodology Summary

The *Creative Success Now* Mindset

Persevere With The Growth Mindset

1. Track your fixed-mindset thoughts and become aware of the situations that trigger your fixed mindset.

2. Create a fixed-mindset persona to see what you are like when the fixed mindset takes over.

3. Affirm your power to change your approach to a growth-mindset approach.

4. Set a growth goal and make a plan to overcome your fixed-mindset challenge.

5. Stretch yourself and take risks. Fixed-mindset people tend to stick with tasks at which they excel; but eventually, they peak.

6. Reach out to trusted mentors and friends when you are stuck.

7. Adopt new strategies to replace old techniques that no longer work. It's a way to work smarter, not necessarily harder.

8. When working on a challenge, remind yourself that you may not be there yet.

9. Set a growth goal and then make a plan and take action steps that will help you achieve your goal.

Get In The Flow With Positivity And Proactivity

1. Recall an experience of flow and embrace the feeling of positivity.

2. Describe what you are like at flow.

3. Take three to five flow words and create your flow affirmation to remind you of what you are like at your best.

4. Tap into your flow self to exude confidence in your creative work.

5. Be proactive by taking action steps toward your dream goal.

6. Spot and create opportunities to make your creative dreams a reality.

7. Experiment and explore new and different fields to generate new possibilities.

The *Creative Success Now* Authenticity Set

Play To Your Passions and Strengths

1. Tap into your creative passion to remember what got you started on your journey.

2. Use your passion to inspire your creative work and inspire others to follow you.

3. Find your strengths by taking the StrengthsFinder 2.0 assessment and writing down five compliments that people give you.

4. Assess how often and how well you use your strengths.

5. Identify the strengths that you do not use enough and make a plan to use them more often and more effectively.

6. Check the strengths that you overuse and dial them down appropriately.

7. Identify the weaknesses that are holding you back and take actions to improve them.

8. Redesign your week to maximize the use of your strengths.

Align with Your Values and Purpose

1. Identify your five top core values.

2. Create your Values Principles.

3. Review your major life decisions to see how well they align with your top values.

4. Redesign your schedule to prioritize your values.

5. When you have a decision to make, see how this decision aligns with your top values. If the decision does not feel quite right, consider what values you may have been ignoring.

6. Write up your seven stories of joy and fulfillment.

7. Imagine your perfect world and how you channel your passions and your best qualities into making the world a better place.

8. Create your Life Purpose Statement.

9. Assess how well your current life is in alignment with your life purpose.

10. Filter your decisions through the lens of your Life Purpose Statement.

11. Engage with the world so that your purpose can find you.

The *Creative Success Now* Skill Sets

Set And Achieve Your Creative Goals

1. Start by creating an inspiring goal—one that you are excited to accomplish by tapping into a vision, using the Creative Career Options Wheel or setting an exploration goal.

2. Break down your goal using the SMART goal process.

3. Line up your strengths and leverage your opportunities to help you achieve your goal.

4. Identify your challenges and strategize how to overcome the challenges.

5. Commit to experimenting when you are not sure of your goal.

6. Take weekly action steps toward your goal.

7. Learn from what is not working, as well as building on what is succeeding.

Overcome The Three Top Creativity Killers

1. Identify your top fear(s) and specify the nature and source of your fear(s).

2. Weigh the evidence that says you are a failure.

3. Learn from your setbacks.

4. Practice success through small victories.

5. Address perfectionism by changing your negative thoughts.

6. Reframe your attitude toward needing perfection in order to succeed.

7. Celebrate your accomplishments.

8. Refrain from comparing yourself to others.

9. Manage your fear of uncertainty.

10. Set a growth goal to overcome your creative block and focus on getting better, not being good.

11. Consider your tolerance for rejection and what you are learning from that experience.

Time Management For Creatives

1. Identify the most important areas of your life and set your top life goals.

2. Set short-term priorities that tie into your important life goals.

3. Create a master to-do list of everything in your professional and personal lives.

4. Sort through your to-do list and slot each activity into one of the four quadrants.

5. Identify your Quadrant Two activities and review your list every month.

6. Review your Quadrant One list and identify which activities contribute to building your Q2.

7. Reduce Quadrant Three activities and eliminate Quadrant Four activities.

8. Plan weekly to slot in Q2 activities and make a strategic, prioritized daily to-do list.

9. Focus on high-impact activities.

10. Minimize external distractions.

11. Say no without apology to activities that are not your priority.

12. Be mindful when you engage in your chosen activities.

13. Figure out why you procrastinate and overcome the temptation to put off doing a difficult or unpleasant task.

Create Your Personal Brand

1. Think about what makes you unique and memorable to the people with whom you work.

2. Write down your favorite activities and what they say about you.

3. Create a profile of your target audience members.

4. Consider what your target audience members are looking for that only you can provide.

5. Review your Perfect World and Life Purpose Statement to extract your *why*.

6. Connect your *why* to your audience's *why*.

7. Write your brand statement.

8. Choose a logo, colors, fonts, and design to exemplify your brand on your website and all written materials.

9. Build your brand and connect with your target audience on social and traditional media.

10. Showcase photos and headshots that convey your brand.

11. Use your brand to inspire your creative work.

Enjoy Networking

1. Examine your attitude toward networking and how it has impacted your career.

2. Decide whom you would like to include in your professional circle and plan your networking strategy.

3. Develop your database of contacts.

4. Create your elevator pitches.

5. Consider what opportunities you have to meet new people and proactively begin to network.

6. Tap into your strengths and passions the next time you meet someone new.

7. Use your flow affirmation to adopt a positive attitude in networking situations.

8. Practice using your elevator pitch when you meet someone with whom you sense a connection.

9. Consider what information, contacts, and resources you can share with people in your network.

10. Follow up with your new contacts and keep them informed of your activities.

11. Be patient as you develop your network and focus on the long-term benefits of having a mutually supportive circle of professional contacts.

12. Conduct an informational interview with someone whose career you admire.

Sustain Your Creative Life

1. Examine your attitude toward your finances and discover what is holding you back.

2. Become financially literate.

3. Create a budget and spending plan.

4. Consider how you can generate revenues as a creative.

5. Start saving and investing.

6. Make your financial plan and begin tracking it against your assumptions and calculations.

7. Form a personal board of directors and reach out to your board members for advice and support.

8. Create a mastermind group with similarly situated creative professionals.

9. Hire a coach for individual coaching.

10. Start a coaching group with like-minded creative professionals and hire a coach to facilitate the sessions.

Your *Creative Success Now* Growth Plan

Creativity is a lifelong journey because creative people are never done. The trick is to keep those big dreams close to your heart and mind and then proactively take the actions to make those dreams a reality. Here's how you can keep the momentum going forward on your lifelong creative journey, using the following system of yearly, monthly, weekly and daily check-ins and planning:

Yearly

Every year, check in with yourself. Think of the yearly assessment as a top-line, big-picture review of what's going well and what needs improvement. Good times to do an annual reflection are January 1, your birthday, the start of a new semester or a new season, or any other logical benchmark from which to launch your yearly review.

Conduct your yearly assessment as follows.

Step One: Gather the assessment materials. First, download the Creative Success Roadmap (creativesuccessnow.com/Creative SuccessRoadmap) and the Creative Life Balance Circle (creativesuccess now.com/balance) from my website.

Step Two: Complete your initial assessment. Next, review and rate each area of the Creative Success Roadmap and the Creative Life

Balance Circle to see where you are in your life. You can track your progress by comparing your assessments to those you completed in chapters 2 and 9.

Step Three: Now it's time to do some writing. Start by examining what is working in your life and then turn to your challenges. Read your flow affirmation to remind you of what you are capable at your optimal best. By focusing on the positive aspects of your life, you are cultivating optimism to help you observe and reflect on areas that need improvement.

What's Working

- What's going well?
- What successes have you experienced?
- Where have you improved?

What Needs Work

- What would you like to improve?
- What challenges are you facing?

It also helps to check in with the elements that define your authentic self.

Authenticity Check-in:

- How passionate are you about your life?
- How aligned are you with your values and principles?
- How well are you using your strengths?
- To what extent does your life feel in alignment with your purpose?

Next, it helps to reflect on your top-level goals.

Goals Check-in

- What progress have you made toward your big goals?
- How committed are you to your big goals and what changes, if any, do you want to make in your goals?

- What are your obstacles to creative success and what have you done to overcome those blocks?

- What challenges do you continue to face in working toward your goals?

Finally, examine your priorities and your short-term goals.

Priorities

- What are the most important things in your life for the coming year (i.e., what's in your Quadrant Two)?

- How well are you incorporating activities from your Quadrant Two?

- What changes do you want to make?

By assessing your progress and your learning, you are incorporating the growth mindset into your life.

Step Four: Set your big goals for the coming year.

Monthly

Create your list of Q2s for the month. You want to make sure that you are proactively taking actions toward those big dreams. Moreover, scan your world for opportunities to make your dreams happen. In this way, you are building proactivity into your system.

Check in on your progress toward achieving your big goals. Document your progress and reflect on what you have learned. Make any necessary changes to your goals.

Weekly

Do a weekly plan to slot in specific action steps that incorporate your Q2s and your goals.

Daily

Make a strategic daily to-do list so that you are meeting your commitments, taking care of Q2s and working toward your goals.

I recommend keeping a journal to track your progress. In my journals, I write down my values, strengths and life purpose statement on the inside cover so that these key elements are ever-present. I also keep a bullet journal to track my monthly Q2s and my daily to-dos. Find a system that works for you. Throughout your journaling and check-ins, be sure to celebrate your successes. Our brains are wired to spot danger, and it is often said we need five positive messages to counter one negative message.

How To Recharge Your Career Satisfaction

S ometimes, we hit a wall. We feel stuck, and we don't know how to move forward.

As you are doing your check-ins, what seems to be out of balance? A good place to start is with your goals. How well do they continue to resonate with your big life plans? Is your intuition telling you to do something else? Is something not working? Do you need some new ideas?

It happens all the time. If that sounds like you, you may need a creative recharge.

As we saw in chapter one, creativity is a problem-solving process. If you think of your stalled creative life as a problem to solve, you can use creativity to generate some new ideas and solutions.

Here are five strategies to help you come up with new ways of thinking about your life.

1. Define your problem

The first step in applying creativity to solve the problem of how to derive more satisfaction is to zero in on what the problem is. For example, you may be stuck by a lack of knowledge and experience. Or you may not have opportunities to play to your strengths. Or your current situation does not align with your values or your purpose. Or you simply do not have the confidence to go after your big dream. Each one of these challenges will involve a different solution.

To find the right problem, you can use a three-step process:

1. Envision your ideal.

2. Asses the reality of your current situation to zero in on the real challenge you are facing.

3. Once you have identified the real challenge, frame your problem as a question: How might I _____ ¿

2. Ideate

Next, have some fun to come up with a lot of wild, wonderful, and even crazy ideas, using a process known as ideation. Ideation is what many people think of as creativity. Ideation sparks your imagination to help you think in a different way. This, in turn, paves the way to more innovative and satisfying ideas.

3. Get new and multiple inputs

Enough thinking. It's time to move to action. That's where you can start applying creativity in your creative life and getting feedback on your ideas.

Too often, we get locked into seeing the world through our current experience. Instead, go out into the field and gather new inputs from multiple sources, including your personal board of directors, informational interviews, networking, and exploring some new areas of interest.

4. Conduct life experiments

Along with gathering new inputs, you can use your creativity to investigate different possibilities. Whether you are in transition, looking to improve your knowledge or skills, interested in increasing your impact or assuming a leadership role, or wishing to gain more confidence, go out and investigate what you are like in a different role by conducting life experiments. Suggestions include volunteering at a local organization, taking a class in a new area, starting a blog about your passion or area of expertise, and shadowing a friend at work.

5. Incubate

The process of addressing your creative life challenges is by no means linear. In fact, this is another area where time is your friend, and it is an essential feature in applying creativity to your life.

Have you ever found yourself grappling with a difficult problem and then leaving your desk in disgust and frustration, only to find the answer when you wake up the next morning or when you are out for a nice walk? Welcome to incubation: one of the magical elements of the creativity process, in which you work hard on a problem, give it time to evolve, and allow new ideas to unfold as a result of your hard work. Incubation does not just happen. Incubation requires preparation so that the elements of a great idea are in place.

If you allow your new inputs to marinate, you will be surprised by how giving yourself permission to incubate will enhance your thinking.

Appendix F

Works Referenced

Achor, Shawn. *The Happiness Advantage: The Seven Principles of Positive Psychology That Fuel Success and Performance at Work*. New York: Broadway Books, 2010.

Amabile, Theresa. "In Pursuit of Everyday Creativity." Working Paper, 2017. http://www.hbs.edu/faculty/Publication%20Files/18-002_ee708f75-293f-4494-bf93-df5cd96b48a6.pdf.

Andreasen, N. C. "Creativity and Mental Illness: Prevalence Rates in Writers and Their First-Degree Relatives." *The American Journal of Psychiatry*. U.S. National Library of Medicine, October 1987. https://www.ncbi.nlm.nih.gov/pubmed/3499088.

Baas, Matthijs, Carsten K W De Dreu, and Bernard A Nijstad. "A Meta-Analysis of 25 Years of Mood-Creativity Research: Hedonic Tone, Activation, or Regulatory Focus?" *Psychological Bulletin*. U.S. National Library of Medicine, November 2008. https://www.ncbi.nlm.nih.gov/pubmed/18954157.

Bach, David. The Latte Factor. https://davidbach.com/latte-factor/.

Berkun, Scott. "Edison Did Not Invent the Lightbulb (The Myth of The Lone Inventor)." Scott Berkun, January 27, 2015. http://scottberkun.com/2015/edison-and-the-light-bulb/.

Bernstein, William J. "If You Can: How Millennials Get Rich Slowly." www.etf.com, 2014. https://www.etf.com/docs/IfYouCan.pdf.

Berrios, Janette. "How To Advance Your Music Career In A Digital Age - MTT." Music Think Tank, http://www.musicthinktank.com/blog/how-to-advance-your-music-career-in-a-digital-age.html.

Biswas-Diener, Robert, Todd B. Kashdan, and Gurpal Minhas. "A Dynamic Approach to Psychological Strength Development and Intervention." Taylor & Francis. April 5, 2011. https://www.tandfonline.com/doi/abs/10.1080/17439760.2010.545429.

Cain, Susan. Quiet—The Power of Introverts in a World That Can`t Stop Talking. New York, NY: Broadway Books, 2013.

Ceciliano, Luke. "There Will Be Fewer Law Firms After 2017 | Attorney Jobs." SEO for Lawyers, LLC, February 7, 2017. https://www.seo-for-lawyers.com/there-will-be-fewer-law-firms-after-2017/.

Chung, Vicky. "A Virtual Crash Course in Design Thinking." Stanford d.school. Stanford d.school, February 5, 2018. https://dschool.stanford.edu/resources-collections/a-virtual-crash-course-in-design-thinking.

Connor, Steve. "The Core of Truth behind Sir Isaac Newton's Apple." The Independent. Independent Digital News and Media, January 18, 2010. https://www.independent.co.uk/news/science/the-core-of-truth-behind-sir-isaac-newtons-apple-1870915.html.

"Conversation with David Lang: Creativity, Entrepreneurship and What It Means to Be an Artist in the 21st Century." Astrid Baumgardner, September 26, 2013. https://www.astridbaumgardner.com/blog-and-resources/blog/conversation-with-david-lang-creativity-entrepreneurship-and-what-it-means-to-be-an-artist-in-the-21st-century/).

Covey, Stephen R. *The 7 Habits of Highly Effective People*. New York, NY: Free Press, 2004.

"Creative Studies, M.S." SUNY Buffalo State. https://suny.buffalostate.edu/programs?bpid=14.

Csikszentmihalyi, Mihaly. *Flow: The Psychology of Optimal Experience*. New York, NY: HarperCollins, 1990.

Csikszentmihalyi, Mihalyi. "The Creative Personality." *Psychology Today*. Sussex Publishers. Accessed March 13, 2019. https://www.psychologytoday.com/us/articles/199607/the-creative-personality.

Dobrow, Shoshanna R., and Daniel Heller. "Siren Song? A Longitudinal Study of the Facilitating Role of Calling and Ability in the Pursuit of a Challenging Career." LSE Research Online. April 2016. http://eprints.lse.ac.uk/65985/1/__lse.ac.uk_storage_LIBRARY_Secondary_libfile_shared_repository_Content_Dobrow%20Riza,%20S_A%20SIREN%20SONG%20A%20LONGITUDI-NAL%20STUDY_Dobrow_Siren_Song.pdf.

Dweck, Carol S. *Mindset: The New Psychology of Success*. New York, NY: Random House, 2016.

Dweck, Carol. "Carol Dweck Revisits the 'Growth Mindset.'" *Education Week*, September 22, 2015. https://www.edweek.org/ew/articles/2015/09/23/carol-dweck-revisits-the-growth-mindset.html.

Dweck, Carol. "Transcript of 'The Power of Believing That You Can Improve.'" TED, https://www.ted.com/talks/carol_dweck_the_power_of_believing_that_you_can_improve/transcript?language=en#t-607761.

Erickson, Kevin. "Musicians and the Digital Age." *Allegro*. Associated Musicians of Greater New York, American Federation of Musicians–Local 802, October 2015. https://www.local802afm.org/allegro/articles/musicians-and-the-digital-age/).

Florida, Richard. *The Rise of the Creative Class—Revisited: 10th Anniversary Edition*, 38–39. New York, NY: Basic Books, 2012.

"42 Revenue Streams." List on Artist Revenue Streams project website (by The Future of Music Coalition). http://money.futureofmusic.org/40-revenue-streams/. http://money.futureofmusic.org/40-revenue-streams/.

Gelfand, Janelle. "Inside a Symphony Audition." Cincinnati.com, November 24, 2015. https://www.cincinnati.com/story/entertainment/music/2015/11/24/inside-symphony-audition/75478764/.

"Goals Research Summary." Dominican University, https://www.dominican.edu/academics/lae/undergraduate-programs/psych/faculty/assets-gail-matthews/researchsummary2.pdf.

Halvorson, Heidi Grant-. *Nine Things Successful People Do Differently*. Boston: Harvard Business Review Press, 2011.

Harsh, Anurag. "The Digital Revolution and Its Impact on Industry, Consumers, and Government." *The Huffington Post*, August 11, 2016. https://www.huffingtonpost.com/entry/the-digital-revolution-and-its-impact-on-industry-consumers_us_57acdc9de-4b0ae60ff020c2d.

Hill, Napoleon. *Think and Grow Rich*. New York, NY: TarcherPerigee, 2005.

Ibarra, Herminia. *Working Identity: Unconventional Strategies for Reinventing Your Career*. Boston, MA: Harvard Business School Press, 2004.

"IBM 2010 Global CEO Study: Creativity Selected as Most Crucial Factor for Future Success." IBM News Room. https://www-03. ibm.com/press/us/en/pressrelease/31670.wss.

Johnson, Steven. "The Creative Apocalypse That Wasn't." *The New York Times*, August 19, 2015. https://www.nytimes.com/2015/08/23/ magazine/the-creative-apocalypse-that-wasnt.html.

Kaufman, Scott Barry. "The Real Neuroscience of Creativity." *Scientific American*, Beautiful Minds column. August 19, 2013. https://blogs. scientificamerican.com/beautiful-minds/the-real-neuroscience-of-creativity/.

Locke, Edwin, T. M. Amabile, and C. M. Fisher. "Stimulate Creativity by Fueling Passion." Essay. In *Handbook of Principles of Organizational Behavior: Indispensable Knowledge for Evidence-Based Management*, 2nd ed., 481–97. West Sussex, UK: John Wiley & Sons, 2009.

Loudenback, Tanza. "25 High-Paying Jobs for Creative Thinkers." *Business Insider*, April 17, 2018. https://www.businessinsider. com/high-paying-jobs-for-creative-thinkers-2016-4#poet-lyricist-or-creative-writer-7.

Lucey, Bill. "Shattering the Myths of Wolfgang Amadeus Mozart." NewspaperAlum, November 5, 2013. http://www.newspaper-alum.com/2013/11/shattering-the-myths-of-wolfgang-amade-us-mozart.html.

Lyubomirsky, Sonja. *The How of Happiness: A New Approach to Getting the Life You Want*. New York, NY: Penguin Books, 2008.

"MacArthur Fellows Frequently Asked Questions." MacArthur Foundation. https://www.macfound.org/fellows-faq/.

Maxwell, John C. *Sometimes You Win—Sometimes You Learn: Life's Greatest Lessons Are Gained from Our Losses.* New York: Center Street, 2015.

"Meet General Director Barbara Lynne Jamison." KY Opera, August 20, 2018. https://kyopera.org/meet-general-director-barbara-lynne-jamison/.

Miedaner, Talane. *Coach Yourself to Success: 101 Tips from a Personal Coach for Reaching Your Goals at Work and in Life.* Lincolnwood, IL: Contemporary Books, 2000.

Moskowitz, Gordon B., and Heidi Grant-Halvorson. *The Psychology of Goals.* New York: Guilford Press, 2009.

"Music 621—Careers in Music: Creating Value Through Innovative Artistic Projects." Yale School of Music Bulletin, July 25, 2018. https://bulletin.yale.edu/sites/default/files/school-of-music-2018-2019.pdf. pp. 64-65.

Peters, Tom. "The Brand Called You." *Fast Company*, August 13, 1997. https://www.fastcompany.com/28905/brand-called-you.

Rath, Tom. *Are You Fully Charged?: The 3 Keys to Energizing Your Work and Life.* Arlington, VA: Silicon Guild, an imprint of Missionday, 2015.

Rath, Tom. *StrengthsFinder 2.0.* Washington, DC: Gallup Press, 2007.

Santiago, José, and World Economic Forum. "What Is Creativity Worth to the World Economy?" World Economic Forum, https://www.weforum.org/agenda/2015/12/creative-industries-worth-world-economy/.

Nicola S. Schutte & John M. Malouff, 2019. "The Impact of Signature Character Strengths Interventions: A Meta-analysis," *Journal of Happiness Studies*, Springer, vol. 20(4), pages 1179-1196, April.

Sinek, Simon. *Start with Why: How Great Leaders Inspire Everyone to Take Action*. London: Portfolio/Penguin, 2013.

Sinek, Simon. "How Great Leaders Inspire Action." TED. https://www.ted.com/talks/simon_sinek_how_great_leaders_inspire_action?language=en.

StrengthsFinder 2.0. Gallup, https://www.gallupstrengthscenter.com/home/en-us/strengthsfinder.

The Imagination Institute. http://www.imagination-institute.org/.

360 Degrees of Financial Literacy, a website of the American Institute of Certified Public Accountants (CPAs). https://www.360financialliteracy.org/.

Tracy, Brian. *Eat That Frog! 21 Great Ways to Stop Procrastinating and Get More Done in Less Time*. Oakland: Barrett-Koehler Pub. Inc., 2017.

University of Indiana. "Strategic National Arts Alumni Project." SNAAP, http://snaap.indiana.edu/pdf/SNAAP_infographics.pdf.

"Unlocking the Power of Introverts." Quiet Revolution. https://www.quietrev.com/.

World Economic Forum. "2022 Skills Outlook." Future of Jobs 2018. http://reports.weforum.org/future-of-jobs-2018/shareable-infographics/.

Wrzesniewski, Amy, Clark McCauley, Paul Rozin, and Barry Schwartz. "Jobs, Careers, and Callings: People's Relations to Their Work." *Journal of Research in Personality*. Retrieved from: Yale.edu., http://faculty.som.yale.edu/amywrzesniewski/documents/Jobscareersandcallings.pdf.

APPENDIX G

Index

Notes

Prologue

[1] "MacArthur Fellows Frequently Asked Questions," MacArthur Foundation, https://www.macfound.org/fellows-faq/.

[2] Ibid.

[3] Mihalyi Csikszentmihalyi, "The Creative Personality," *Psychology Today* (Sussex Publishers), https://www.psychologytoday.com/us/articles/199607/the-creative-personality.

Chapter 1

[1] "IBM 2010 Global CEO Study: Creativity Selected as Most Crucial Factor for Future Success," IBM News Room , accessed May 13, 2019, https://www-03.ibm.com/press/us/en/pressrelease/31670.wss

[2] World Economic Forum, "2022 Skills Outlook," accessed March 13, 2019, http://reports.weforum.org/future-of-jobs-2018/shareable-infographics/.

[3] Richard Florida, *The Rise of the Creative Class—Revisited: 10th Anniversary Edition* (New York, NY: Basic Books, 2012), 38-39.

[4] Connor, Steve, "The Core of Truth behind Sir Isaac Newton's Apple," The Independent, Independent Digital News and Media, January 18, 2010. https://www.independent.co.uk/news/science/the-core-of-truth-behind-sir-isaac-newtons-apple-1870915.html.

[5] Bill Lucey, "Shattering the Myths of Wolfgang Amadeus Mozart," NewspaperAlum, November 5, 2013, http://www.newspaperalum.com/2013/11/shattering-the-myths-of-wolfgang-amadeus-mozart.html.

[6] Scott Berkun, "Edison Did Not Invent the Lightbulb (The Myth of The Lone Inventor)," Scott Berkun.com, January 27, 2015, http://scottberkun.com/2015/edison-and-the-light-bulb/.

[7] Scott Barry Kaufman, "The Real Neuroscience of Creativity," *Scientific American*, Beautiful Minds column, August 19, 2013, https://blogs.

scientificamerican.com/beautiful-minds/the-real-neuroscience-of-creativity/.

[8] The Imagination Institute, http://www.imagination-institute.org/.

[9] Kaufman, "The Real Neuroscience of Creativity."

[10] "Conversation with David Lang: Creativity, Entrepreneurship and What It Means to Be an Artist in the 21st Century," Astrid Baumgardner, September 26, 2013, https://www.astridbaumgardner.com/blog-and-resources/blog/conversation-with-david-lang-creativity-entrepreneurship-and-what-it-means-to-be-an-artist-in-the-21st-century/).

[11] Interview, Reena Esmail, April 19, 2019. Reena is an Indian-American composer who works between the worlds of Indian and Western classical music. http://www.reenaesmail.com.

[12] Vicky Chung, "A Virtual Crash Course in Design Thinking," Stanford d.school (Stanford d.school, February 5, 2018), https://dschool.stanford.edu/resources-collections/a-virtual-crash-course-in-design-thinking.

[13] "Creative Studies, M.S.," SUNY Buffalo State, https://suny.buffalostate.edu/programs?bpid=14.

[14] "Music 621—Careers in Music: Creating Value Through Innovative Artistic Projects," Yale School of Music Bulletin, July 25, 2018, pp. 64-65. https://bulletin.yale.edu/sites/default/files/school-of-music-2018-2019.pdf.

[15] N. C. Andreasen, "Creativity and Mental Illness: Prevalence Rates in Writers and Their First-Degree Relatives," *The American Journal of Psychiatry* (U.S. National Library of Medicine, October 1987), https://www.ncbi.nlm.nih.gov/pubmed/3499088.

[16] Lyubomirsky, Sonja. *The How of Happiness: A New Approach to Getting the Life You Want*. New York, NY: Penguin Books, 2008, 32.

[17] Theresa Amabile, "In Pursuit of Everyday Creativity," Working Paper, 2017, http://www.hbs.edu/faculty/Publication Files/18-002_ee708f75-293f-4494-bf93-df5cd96b48a6.pdf.

[18] Matthijs Baas, Carsten K W De Dreu, and Bernard A Nijstad, "A Meta-Analysis of 25 Years of Mood-Creativity Research: Hedonic Tone, Activation, or Regulatory Focus?," *Psychological Bulletin* (U.S. National Library of Medicine, November 2008), https://www.ncbi.nlm.nih.gov/pubmed/18954157.

[19] Mihaly Csikszentmihalyi, *Flow: the Psychology of Optimal Experience* (New York, NY: HarperCollins, 1990), 208-213.

[20] Sonja Lyubomirsky, *The How of Happiness*, 181-190.

[21] Janelle Gelfand, "Inside a Symphony Audition," Cincinnati.com, November 24, 2015, https://www.cincinnati.com/story/entertainment/music/2015/11/24/inside-symphony-audition/75478764/.

[22] Shoshanna R. Dobrow and Daniel Heller, "Siren Song? A Longitudinal Study of the Facilitating Role of Calling and Ability in the Pursuit of a Challenging Career," LSE Research Online, http://eprints.lse.ac.uk/65985/1/__lse.ac.uk_storage_LIBRARY_Secondary_libfile_shared_repository_Content_Dobrow Riza, S_A SIREN SONG A LONGITUDINAL STUDY_Dobrow_Siren_Song.pdf.

[23] Csikszentmihalyi, "The Creative Personality."

[24] Lyubomirsky, *The How of Happiness*, chapter 8.

[25] University of Indiana, "Strategic National Arts Alumni Project," SNAAP, http://snaap.indiana.edu/pdf/SNAAP_infographics.pdf. SNAAP collects data from alumni of twelve creative fields: design, fine and studio art, art history and curatorial studies, music, media arts, theater, arts education, architecture, crafts, dance, arts administration, and creative writing. Ninety-one percent of alumni rated their educational experience as "positive;" 70 percent work in arts-related fields; 88 percent are satisfied with their work.

[26] Luke Ceciliano, "There Will Be Fewer Law Firms After 2017 | Attorney Jobs," SEO for Lawyers, LLC, February 7, 2017, https://www.seo-for-lawyers.com/there-will-be-fewer-law-firms-after-2017/.

[27] Steven Johnson, "The Creative Apocalypse That Wasn't," *The New York Times*, August 19, 2015, https://www.nytimes.com/2015/08/23/magazine/the-creative-apocalypse-that-wasnt.html.

[28] UNCTAD, the UN Conference on Trade and Development, formed the Creative Economy Programme to analyze and study the global creative economy and its impact on developing countries. The programme explains that the creative economy is an "evolving concept" that "builds on the interplay between human creativity and ideas and intellectual property, knowledge and technology" and observes that the creative industries are "an important source of commercial and cultural value." https://unctad.org/en/Pages/DITC/CreativeEconomy/Creative-Economy-Programme.aspx accessed on August 6, 2019.

[29] José Santiago and World Economic Forum, "What Is Creativity Worth to the World Economy?," World Economic Forum, https://www.weforum.org/agenda/2015/12/creative-industries-worth-world-economy/. According to this report, conducted by Ernst & Young and jointly presented by UNESCO and the International Confederation of Authors and Composers Societies (CISAC), the top three employers are visual arts (6.73 million employees), books (3.67 million) and music (3.98 million).

[30] Tanza Loudenback, "25 High-Paying Jobs for Creative Thinkers," *Business Insider*, April 17, 2018, https://www.businessinsider.com/high-paying-jobs-for-creative-thinkers-2016-4#poet-lyricist-or-creative-writer-7.

[31] University of Indiana, "Strategic National Arts Alumni Project," SNAAP, http://snaap.indiana.edu/pdf/SNAAP_infographics.pdf.

[32] Anurag Harsh, "The Digital Revolution and Its Impact on Industry, Consumers, and Government," *The Huffington Post*, August 11, 2016, https://www.huffingtonpost.com/entry/the-digital-revolution-and-its-impact-on-industry-consumers_us_57acdc9de4b0ae60ff020c2d.

[33] Johnson, "The Creative Apocalypse That Wasn't."

[34] Janette Berrios, "How To Advance Your Music Career In A Digital

Age - MTT," Music Think Tank, http://www.musicthinktank.com/blog/how-to-advance-your-music-career-in-a-digital-age.html.

[35] Kevin Erickson, "Musicians and the Digital Age." *Allegro*. Associated Musicians of Greater New York, American Federation of Musicians–Local 802, October 2015. https://www.local802afm.org/allegro/articles/musicians-and-the-digital-age/).

Chapter 2

[1] For a good summary of happiness research, see *The Happiness Advantage: The Seven Principles of Positive Psychology That Fuel Success and Performance at Work* (New York: Crown Business, 2010) by Shawn Achor. Dr. Achor was a Harvard researcher and head teaching fellow in one of the most popular courses at Harvard called "Happiness." He now is the founder and CEO of Aspirant, a research and consulting company that uses positive psychology to help individuals and organizations enhance their achievement and cultivate a more positive workplace.

[2] Lyubomirsky, *The How of Happiness*, 20-22.

Part I

[1] Sō Percussion, https://sopercussion.com/. The "Sō" in Sō Percussion comes from a Japanese word that means "to play an instrument." But it can also mean "to be successful," "to determine a direction and move forward," and "to present to the gods or ruler."

Chapter 3

[1] tonebase, https://tonebase.co.

[2] Carol S. Dweck, *Mindset: The New Psychology of Success* (New York, NY: Random House, 2016).

[3] Dweck, *Mindset*, 42-43. Dweck illustrates the challenge of riding on talent with the story of a world-famous musician, violinist Nadja Salerno-Sonenberg. Salerno-Sonenberg was a child prodigy who made her debut with the Philadelphia Orchestra at age ten and arrived at Juilliard to study with the great violin teacher, Dorothy DeLay. DeLay found that the young violinist had developed terrible habits, which

Salerno-Sonenberg refused to change. As the years went by, other students began to catch up with her, and by the time she was in her late teens, she had a crisis in confidence. She was afraid to try—because if she tried and failed, it would be unbearable to give it her all and then not succeed. Things got so bad that she stopped bringing her violin to lessons, whereupon DeLay announced that she had had enough: "If you are going to waste your talent, I am not going to be a part of it."

The fear of losing DeLay was the wake-up call that Salerno-Sonenberg needed, and she changed her approach: For the first time in her life, she put in 100 percent effort on an upcoming competition. The result was that she won the competition and went on to achieve the fame that she enjoys today—all with a lot of hard work.

4 Carol Dweck, "Carol Dweck Revisits the 'Growth Mindset'," *Education Week*, September 22, 2015, https://www.edweek.org/ew/articles/2015/09/23/carol-dweck-revisits-the-growth-mindset.html.

5 Dweck, *Mindset*. pp. 257-60.

6 See discussion of get better goals in Chapter 8.

7 Carol Dweck, "Transcript of 'The Power of Believing That You Can Improve,'" TED, https://www.ted.com/talks/carol_dweck_the_power_of_believing_that_you_can_improve/transcript?language=en#t-607761.

Dr. Dweck was inspired by a high school in Chicago where students who did not master a subject matter were given the grade "not yet." This kind of thinking overcomes the notion that "I will never get this," or "I am too dumb to get this."

Chapter 4

7 Shawn Achor, *The Happiness Advantage: The Seven Principles of Positive Psychology That Fuel Success and Performance at Work* (New York: Broadway Books, 2010), 14-15.

8 Lyubomirsky, *The How of Happiness*, 20-22.

9 Csikszentmihalyi, *Flow*.

10 Csikszentmihalyi, *Flow*, 208-213.

[11] "Opera America Leadership Intensive," OPERA America, https://operaamerica.org/content/about/leadint.aspx.

[12] "Meet General Director Barbara Lynne Jamison," KY Opera, August 20, 2018, https://kyopera.org/meet-general-director-barbara-lynne-jamison/.

[13] Liquid Theatre Collective, http://liquidtheatrecollective.org

[14] Bang on a Can, https://bangonacan.org

[15] I participated in a panel discussion with David Lang and Michael Gordon on June 22, 2018, in which the two founders discussed the early years of Bang on a Can. See https://www.astridbaumgardner.com/blog-and-resources/bang-on-a-can-inspiring-innovation-experimentation-entrepreneurship/

Chapter 5

[1] Tillid Group, http://tillidgroup.com/.

[2] Edwin Locke, T. M. Amabile, and C. M. Fisher, "Stimulate Creativity by Fueling Passion," essay, in *Handbook of Principles of Organizational Behavior: Indispensable Knowledge for Evidence-Based Management, 2nd ed.* (West Sussex, UK: John Wiley & Sons, 2009), 481-497.

[3] Nicola S. Schutte & John M. Malouff. "The Impact of Signature Character Strengths Interventions: A Meta-analysis," *Journal of Happiness Studies*, Springer, vol. 20(4), pages 1179-1196, April, 2019.

[4] Tom Rath, *StrengthsFinder 2.0* (Washington, DC: Gallup Press, 2007), 18-22.

[5] Robert Biswas-Diener, Todd B. Kashdan, and Gurpal Minhas. "A Dynamic Approach to Psychological Strength Development and Intervention," *Taylor & Francis*, accessed April 5, 2011, https://www.tandfonline.com/doi/abs/10.1080/17439760.2010.545429.

[6] Schutte, N. S., & Malouff, J. M. "The Impact of Signature Character Strengths Interventions:: A meta-analysis."

[7] "StrengthsFinder 2.0," Gallup, https://www.gallupstrengthscenter.com/home/en-us/strengthsfinder.

[8] Tom Rath, *StrengthsFinder 2.0*

[9] Ibid.

Chapter 6
[1] Gelfand, "Inside a Symphony Audition."

[2] Tom Rath, *Are You Fully Charged? The 3 Keys to Energizing Your Work and Life* (Arlington, VA: Silicon Guild, an imprint of Missionday, 2015), 39

[3] Amy Wrzesniewski et al., "Jobs, Careers, and Callings: People's Relations to Their Work," *Journal of Research in Personality*, retrieved from http://faculty.som.yale.edu/amywrzesniewski/documents/Jobscareersandcallings.pdf, 21-33.

[4] Ibid.

[5] I gratefully acknowledge Master Certified Coach Teri-E Belf and the Success Unlimited Network for inspiration and guidance in teaching me the SUN Life Purpose Facilitation process. http://www.belfcoach.com. I have adapted these principles to create my own process for creatives.

Chapter 7
[1] Street Symphony, http://streetsymphony.org

[2] Shastra, http://shastramusic.org

[3] Reena Esmail, http://www.reenaesmail.com/bio/

[4] The Shiu Clinic, https://www.shiuclinic.com

[5] I am indebted to my coaching program, the Institute for Professional Excellence in Coaching or iPEC (https://www.ipeccoaching.com), for teaching me the principles of goal-setting and how to use wheels to set goals. The Creative Career Options Circle contains my interpretation of the copyrighted work of Bruce D. Schneider and iPEC.

[6] Andrea Kornbluth Prints, http://www.akornbluthprints.com.

[7] Herminia Ibarra, *Working Identity: Unconventional Strategies for Reinventing Your Career* (Boston, MA: Harvard Business School Press, 2004).

[8] "Goals Research Summary," Dominican University, https://www.dominican.edu/academics/lae/undergraduate-programs/psych/faculty/assets-gail-matthews/researchsummary2.pdf.

[9] Sō Percussion Summer Institute, https://sopercussion.com/education/summer-institute/

[10] Missy Mazzoli shared her career path when she participated in a panel of Yale School of Music alumni who spoke at my class at the Yale School of Music in November 2013. http://www.astridbaumgardner.com/blog-and-resources/blog/creating-success-in-a-diy-world-4-ysm-music-entrepreneurs-share-their-insights/

[11] Missy Mazzoli, http://missymazzoli.com

Chapter 8

[1] Jake and I reviewed the principles of the growth mindset that are laid out in chapter 3.

[2] John C. Maxwell, *Sometimes You Win—Sometimes You Learn: Life's Greatest Lessons Are Gained from Our Losses* (New York: Center Street, 2015).

[3] Heidi Grant- Halvorson, *Nine Things Successful People Do Differently* (Boston: Harvard Business Review Press, 2011).

[4] Gordon B. Moskowitz and Heidi Grant-Halvorson, *The Psychology of Goals* (New York: Guilford Press, 2009).

Chapter 9

[1] The Creative Life Balance Circle contains my interpretation of the copyrighted work of Bruce D. Schneider and iPEC.

[2] Stephen R Covey, *The 7 Habits of Highly Effective People* (New York, NY: Free Press, 2004).

[3] Reprinted with permission from Franklin Covey Co.

[4] "Ensemble Connect," Ensemble Connect, , https://www.carnegiehall.org/Education/Ensemble-Connect?sourceCode=29598&gclid=EAIaIQobChMIr8Gf1vDj4QIVRVcMCh1oSAGZEAAYASAAEgJRRPD_BwE.

[5] These questions come from Talane Miedaner, *Coach Yourself to Success: 101 Tips from a Personal Coach for Reaching Your Goals at Work and in Life* (Lincolnwood, IL: Contemporary Books, 2000).

[6] Brian Tracy, *Eat That Frog! 21 Great Ways to Stop Procrastinating and Get More Done in Less Time* (Oakland: Berrett-Koehler Publishers, Inc., 3d edition, 2017).

Chapter 10

[1] Florrie Marshall. https://www.florriemarshall.com/. Accessed May 14, 2019.

[2] Tom Peters, "The Brand Called You," Fast Company, August 13, 1997, https://www.fastcompany.com/28905/brand-called-you.

[3] "Argus Quartet." Argus Quartet. http://argusquartet.com/#About.

[4] Simon Sinek, *Start with Why: How Great Leaders Inspire Everyone to Take Action* (London: Portfolio/Penguin, 2013).

[5] Simon Sinek, "How Great Leaders Inspire Action," TED, https://www.ted.com/talks/simon_sinek_how_great_leaders_inspire_action?language=en.

[6] Florrie Marshall, https://www.florriemarshall.com/artist-1, accessed May 13, 2019.

Chapter 11

[1] Adam Schoenberg, http://adamschoenberg.com

[2] Susan Cain, *Quiet—The Power of Introverts in a World That Can't Stop Talking* (New York, NY: Broadway Books, 2013).

[3] "Unlocking the Power of Introverts," Quiet Revolution. https://www.quietrev.com/.

Chapter 12

[1] Mint. https://www.mint.com/?dd_pm=none&dd_pm_cat=finance_app.

[2] I am indebted to my colleague, Steve Blum, Senior Director, Strategic Initiatives of the Yale Alumni Association and Resident Fellow, Branford College, Yale University, for his brilliant workshop, "Financial Life After Yale," that has helped thousands of Yale graduates to manage their finances.

[3] Bach, David. The Latte Factor. https://davidbach.com/latte-factor/.

[4] 360 Degrees of Financial Literacy, a website of the American Institute of Certified Public Accountants (CPAs), accessed March 13, 2019, https://www.360financialliteracy.org/.

[5] Bernstein, William J. "If You Can: How Millennials Get Rich Slowly." www.etf.com, 2014. https://www.etf.com/docs/IfYouCan.pdf.

[6] Fidelity, Vanguard, and Charles Schwab websites:
   Fidelity Investments, https://www.fidelity.com/
   Vanguard Investments, https://investor.vanguard.com/
   Charles Schwab, https://www.schwab.com/

[7] The Future of Music Coalition lists 42 revenue streams for performers and composers. http://money.futureofmusic.org/40-revenue-streams/

[8] Christine Carter, http://christine-carter.com

[9] Napoleon Hill, *Think and Grow Rich* (New York, NY: TarcherPerigee, 2005).

Made in the USA
Middletown, DE
09 January 2020

82582688R10123